CAKE, I LOVE YOU

CAKE,
I LOVE YOU

DECADENT, DELECTABLE,
and DO-ABLE RECIPES

Jill O'Connor

Photographs by Leigh Beisch

Illustrations by Jordan Sondler

CHRONICLE BOOKS
SAN FRANCISCO

Library of Congress Cataloging-in-Publication Data:

Names: O'Connor, Jill, author.
Title: Cake, I love you : decadent, delectable, and do-able recipes / Jill O'Connor.
Description: San Francisco : Chronicle Books, 2017. | Includes index.
Identifiers: LCCN 2016025898 | ISBN 9781452153803 (hardback)
Subjects: LCSH: Cake. | BISAC: COOKING / Methods / Baking. |
  COOKING / Courses & Dishes / Cakes. | LCGFT: Cookbooks.
Classification: LCC TX771 .O29 2017 | DDC 641.86/53—dc23 LC record
  available at https://lccn.loc.gov/2016025898

Manufactured in China

Designed by Alice Chau.
Illustrations by Jordan Sondler.

Food styling by Robyn Valarik.
Prop styling by Sara Slavin.

Chronicle books and gifts are available at special quantity discounts to corporations, professional associations, literacy programs, and other organizations. For details and discount information, please contact our premiums department at corporatesales@chroniclebooks.com or at 1-800-759-0190.

10 9 8 7 6 5 4 3 2 1

Chronicle Books LLC
680 Second Street
San Francisco, California 94107
www.chroniclebooks.com

For Olivia and Sophia: You are both my sweet inspiration; every day with the two of you is filled with buttercream and chocolate sprinkles and joy.

For Jim: You make me laugh just as hard today as you did the day I met you— thank you for showing me that with a sense of humor, even life's little catastrophes can be crafted into a delicious story.

And in memory of my father, who taught me that the sweetest recipe for a life well-lived starts with love.

Underlined cakes are crowd-pleaser recipes; see page 9 for details

CAKE: A LOVE STORY

It's no secret that I love cake. At different times, it's been my best friend, my muse, and, when I am on a diet, my kryptonite. I think there is no fragrance more heavenly than the smell of pound cake baking, and that everything good and right and wonderful in the world starts with the words, "cream together the butter and sugar."

I've been baking for as long as I can remember, and my favorite dessert to bake by far has always been cake.

There is something inherently festive and special about a homemade cake, from the simplest loaf of banana cake sprinkled with confectioners' sugar to a towering triple-layer chocolate fudge cake filled with pastry cream and caramel, slathered with buttercream, and dripping in chocolate ganache. I remain convinced that the addition of a cake, no matter how humble, can make the most mundane event feel like a party.

When I was in the second grade, my mother brought home a huge burnt almond cake from our neighborhood bakery to celebrate my first communion. The delicate vanilla-scented cake layers were frosted with a creamy German buttercream—a heart-skipping concoction of rich pastry cream rendered airy and silken by whipping in lots of butter. Encrusted in caramelized almonds, with big white frosting roses crowded into the corners, it was an imposing beauty. But

what impressed me the most was the giant, pressed-sugar chalice brushed with gold, and moonlike communion wafer that floated on top of the cake. I barely remember the important events of the day, but I do remember circling that cake, like a fox circling a chicken coop, through most of my party. I indulged my grandparents as they planted congratulatory kisses on my cheek, but remained transfixed and slightly obsessed—until my mother cut the cake. She handed me a corner piece with a fat frosting rose and another small plate holding the sugar chalice and communion wafer. I was awed, and a bit confused. Do I eat them? Do I save them? Were they, in fact, holy? This last question remained unanswered, as temptation got the better of me and I crunched my way through the chalice by the end of the day. Holy? Well, I saved the communion wafer, wrapped in a cocktail napkin, for about a week, until my mother told me to eat it or throw it away before the ants got to it.

To this day, I still find cake slightly magical, and in all its many flavors, shapes, and sizes, worthy of my obsessive attention. Ever since that transcendent burnt-almond cake, I've realized that in so many of my memories, of both the big events and the little everyday moments, there is usually cake.

I wooed my husband with dark chocolate black-bottom cupcakes while we were dating—their rich, robust exterior hiding

a sweet and creamy cheesecake heart that said more than I could with words at the time. When our daughters were born (their taste buds genetically programmed to adore everything sweet), cake was always a happy part of their everyday lives. For big events like their birthdays, their cakes matched the birthday party theme. There was a chocolate cake shaped like a bowling ball; a lemon sheet cake carved into an artist's palette, complete with colorful dollops of frosting "paint"; and a honey cake shaped like a beehive and frosted in loopy swirls of honey buttercream with little marzipan bees buzzing around it.

When my oldest daughter had to create a 3-D model of an animal cell in sixth grade, I helped her carve it out of cream-cheese pound cake, piping everything from the mitochondria to the ribosomes in colorful royal icing. I think it was the first completely edible cell her teacher had ever seen. When my youngest daughter turned ten and started playing softball, I wanted to participate with the other parents, but my knowledge of the game wouldn't fill a teacup, so I did what I always do—I baked. Every week there were chocolate chip cookies, snickerdoodles, cupcakes, slices of banana bread, or pumpkin muffins, but my most popular offering, hands down, was the New York–style crumb cake I brought to one game—big squares of tender sour-cream coffee cake covered in big chunks of sweet, rocky, brown sugar crumble.

Of course, I am not the only one who thinks a cake equals a party. Birthdays and weddings, graduation days and baby showers wouldn't be the same without a luscious cake bedecked and festooned in layers of buttercream and sprinkles and flowers and candles, holding a place of honor to symbolize the importance of the occasion.

Everyone loves cake, in one form or another, and they always will. Life is too short to live on kale, kombucha, and quinoa alone. This book is my unapologetic love letter to cake, in all its sweet, gorgeous, indulgent, and celebratory glory. In these pages, I serve up an irresistible, eclectic, and multilayered homage to the goodness of cake, with a collection of recipes for baking both simple and elaborate but always delicious and beautiful cakes at home.

The chapters are divided by flavors, focusing on the ones we love most, from banana to coconut to chocolate to caramel to lemon, all dolled up with nuts and spices—and the occasional splash of spirits to make things interesting.

Each flavor-centric chapter begins with a few simple recipes for snack cakes, loaf cakes, coffee cakes, and single-layer cakes, such as the Banana-Butterscotch Loaf (page 27), Hummingbird Morning Cake (page 30), Classic Diner Crumb Cake (page 136), and Kona Coconut Loaf (page 48), that can be stirred together in a matter of minutes. The heart of each chapter is an array of slightly more ambitious creations, from traditional sheet cakes and layer cakes like

Old-Fashioned Chocolate Mayonnaise Cake with Melted Chocolate Bar Frosting (page 74) and Proper Victoria Sponge with Ginger-Roasted Rhubarb and Devonshire-Style Cream (page 163) to exuberant, triple-layer wonders like Classic Southern Caramel Cake (page 102) and Chocolate–Peanut Butter Blackout Cake (page 82), that might require a stand mixer, multiple cake pans—and maybe even a candy thermometer—to produce a dazzling showstopper of a cake that will light up any celebration table.

When you can't decide which cake to make, look for the "crowd-pleaser" stamp of approval. Every chapter features one classic, iconic favorite you can turn to again and again with confidence.

Whether you're looking for an extravagant birthday cake dripping in caramel and covered in chocolate curls or just a simple loaf of lemon cake to serve with your morning coffee, *Cake, I Love You,* has just the right cake, in just the right flavor, for you.

CROWD-PLEASER

BAKER'S GEAR

Here are the tools, equipment, and bakeware you will need to make baking a cake a pleasure in your kitchen.

HEAVY-DUTY EQUIPMENT

FOOD PROCESSOR

Indispensable for chopping nuts and making nut flours, chopping and puréeing fruit, making mayonnaise, and blending simple cake batters.

HAND MIXER

With the exception of meringue buttercreams, every recipe in this book can be successfully prepared with a hand mixer. Even if you have a stand mixer, a hand mixer is a must. Hand mixers are perfect for smaller jobs, and for things like beating egg whites or whipping cream when your stand mixer is already in use.

STAND MIXER

I once joked that I wanted to be buried with my KitchenAid mixer. A stand mixer makes baking so much easier. With paddle and whisk attachments, it is indispensable for making smooth cake batters and for making meringue-based frostings and buttercreams that require a prodigious amount of beating. With the hands-free benefit, you can do more than one thing at a time.

BAKEWARE

BAKING SHEETS

Professional-quality rimmed half-sheet pans (aka baking sheets) (13 by 18 in [33 cm by 46 cm]) are available in kitchenware stores and restaurant supply stores. You'll find them necessary for roasting fruit, toasting nuts, or holding a wire rack when glazing cakes. I like to spread melted chocolate on the back of a rimmed baking sheet pan to make chocolate curls (see page 37). Sheet pans with a nonstick coating are not as versatile and rugged as standard aluminum sheet pans and tend to scratch, so stick with the sturdier, classic aluminum pans.

CAKE PANS

There's no need to buy the most expensive cake pans. Kitchenware, restaurant supply, and craft stores carry a variety of cost-effective, sturdy, lightweight, rustproof aluminum cake pans in various sizes and depths that are easy to clean. It's a good idea to have three pans each in 6-in [15-cm], 8-in [20-cm], and 9-in [23-cm] sizes, for triple-layer cakes. I prefer cake pans without a nonstick coating. They are less expensive and more versatile, appropriate for multiple batters from butter cakes to sponge and chiffon cakes.

All the cakes in this book are made in a few specific pans of various sizes, as follows:

Bundt pan
10- or 12- cup [2.4- or 2.8-L]

Loaf pan
9 by 5 in [23 by 12 cm]

Round pans
6 by 2 in [15 by 5 cm]
8 by 2 in [20 by 5 cm]
9 by 2 in [23 by 5 cm]
9 by 3 in [23 by 7.5 cm]

Square pan
9 in [23 cm]

Sheet pan
9 by 13 in [23 by 33 cm]

Springform pan
9 in [23 cm]

Look for the newer version of this pan, with a wider base and a stronger latch. The new pan is engineered to be leakproof, to accommodate thinner cake batters without any dripping or leaking while baking.

Fluted tart pan with removable bottom
9 or 10 in [23 or 25 cm]

A shallow tart pan is perfect for baking dense, sticky batters like the Raspberry-Hazelnut Financier (page 160). The removable bottom easily supports the cake when you slip off the pan's outer ring.

NONSTICK COOKING/BAKING SPRAYS

I prefer using a very thin film of nonstick cooking spray or nonstick baking spray (an aerosol mixture of oil and flour) to guarantee that my cakes don't stick. Pans that are buttered and floured to prevent sticking can also give the baked cake a tough exterior crust or leave tiny, dry pockets of flour behind in the baked cake.

PARCHMENT PAPER

This is one of the most indispensable tools in cake baking. You can buy it in rolls like foil or plastic wrap or in precut rounds for individual cake pans. It is crucial for ensuring that cakes come out of their pans without sticking.

WIRE COOLING RACKS

Cakes need to be cooled on raised wire racks so that air can circulate to keep the sponge from getting soggy. Racks are also handy for holding cakes over a rimmed baking sheet as you glaze them with ganache and other sauces.

POTS AND PANS

CAST-IRON SKILLET (10 IN [25 CM])

Use on the stovetop to sauté fruit or toast and caramelize nuts, and in the oven for baking upside-down cakes and fruit buckles. I like Lodge cast-iron skillets as well as Le Creuset enameled cast-iron pans.

STAINLESS STEEL–LINED SAUCEPANS

Heavy stainless steel–lined saucepans are worth the investment. I have one each in 1-qt [960-ml], 2-qt [2-L], and 3-qt [2.8-L] sizes. Use them for poaching fruit; making custards, sugar syrups, and caramel sauce; browning butter; and making small quantities of jam or jelly.

STOCKPOT (8 QT [7.5 L])

Necessary for jam making and boiling cans of sweetened condensed milk to make dulce de leche.

CUPS, BOWLS, AND SPOONS

DRY MEASURING CUPS

These sturdy metal or plastic cups do not reflect true volume measurements, so use them for measuring dry ingredients from sugar and flour to cornmeal and chopped or ground nuts. A standard set of dry measuring cups should include ¼-cup [60-ml], ⅓-cup [80-ml], ½-cup [125-ml], and 1-cup [250-ml] scoops.

LIQUID MEASURING CUPS

These come in plastic or Pyrex. It's nice to have at least one each of microwave-safe 2-cup [480-ml] and 4-cup [960-ml] sizes for measuring liquids.

MEASURING SPOONS

Metal or plastic spoons in ¼-tsp, ½-tsp, 1-tsp, and 1-Tbsp amounts.

NESTING PYREX BOWLS

Pyrex bowls are oven-, dishwasher-, and freezer-safe. I place one over a saucepan to make an impromptu double boiler, bake cakes in them, whip small amounts of cream in them, and use them for every other reason one would need a bowl.

STAINLESS-STEEL BOWLS (2 QT [2 L])

These bowls are also oven-, dishwasher-, and freezer-safe, with the added benefit of being very lightweight and easy to clean.

TOOLS

BENCH SCRAPER

In cake baking, I use these for making chocolate curls and smoothing the sides of frosted cakes. Bench scrapers have a flat stainless-steel blade measuring about 6 by 4 in [15 by 10 cm]. They usually have an easy-to-grip rubber or wooden handle.

BLOWTORCH

I use a standard propane blowtorch that I bought at the hardware store, but smaller kitchen torches that run on butane are available from kitchenware stores if a big blowtorch seems intimidating. Use the torch to caramelize sugar and to burnish meringue.

CANDY THERMOMETER

I bought one years ago to make the caramel icing for a caramel cake, and realized that this little tool makes candy making so much less stressful. Candy thermometers are inexpensive, and crucial for measuring the temperature when cooking sugar syrups for caramel, marshmallows, and French and Italian meringue buttercream. They take the guesswork out of the equation, and make the whole process much easier.

DIGITAL SCALE

Weighing ingredients isn't common in American kitchens, but it is a more accurate way to bake. If you want to give it a try, start by weighing your flour; an inaccurate measurement of flour is one of the biggest reasons cakes, especially, turn out heavy or dry. One cup of all-purpose flour weighs 140 grams.

GRATERS AND ZESTER

Box graters and Microplane zesters (both fine and coarse) are used to grate chocolate, fresh coconut, and citrus zest.

KNIVES

A paring knife, an 8- or 10-in [20- or 25-cm] chef's knife, and a 12-in [30.5-cm] serrated bread knife are really all you need. Serrated knives are necessary for splitting cake layers into multiple layers.

SIEVE

Use fine-mesh sieves for sifting dry ingredients together, sprinkling confectioners' sugar over cakes, and straining fruit purées and citrus curds.

SPATULAS

Long, flat, narrow metal spatulas and offset spatulas (flat, narrow metal spatulas with a bend near the handle) in various sizes are my favorite tools for frosting cakes. Offset spatulas follow the curves of the cake and make it easy to get into the nooks and crannies. Heatproof rubber or silicone spatulas are great for stirring, scraping, spreading, and folding ingredients together. You can never have too many.

WIRE WHISKS

I use a variety of wire whisks. Favorites include a large, round balloon whisk for whisking eggs and egg whites and a longer, narrower whisk with stiffer wires, sometimes called a "piano whisk," for beating custards and firmer batters. I also like having a few small whisks for beating a single egg or whisking smaller amounts of ingredients together.

DECORATING TOOLS

CAKE TURNTABLE

Revolving cake stands with a cast-iron base are sturdy and durable. If you want to get really proficient at frosting cakes, they are a necessity. The spinning action makes frosting a cake fast and almost effortless.

CARDBOARD CAKE ROUNDS

Made from corrugated cardboard, single-use cake rounds or cake circles provide sturdy support for layer cakes, and enable you to move the cake from a revolving cake turntable to a cake box or covered cake carrier for traveling, or to a cake plate or cake stand for serving. Look for 6-in [15-cm], 8-in [20-cm], 9-in [23-cm], and 10-in [25-cm] sizes.

DISPOSABLE PIPING BAGS

Disposable piping, or pastry, bags make frosting and decorating easy. Both 12-in [30.5-cm] and 16-in [40.5-cm] bags are handy to have on hand.

BAKER'S PANTRY

Every baker will tell you, the most delicious cakes start with the finest ingredients. Use fruits and vegetables when they are in season and at their best and most flavorful; real butter; pure cane sugar; fresh eggs; and the best cocoa and chocolate you can find. Here is a list of the ingredients I like to have on hand whenever I start baking.

ALMOND FLOUR AND ALMOND MEAL

Almond flour is made from very finely ground blanched almonds. Almond meal is made from finely ground roasted whole almonds (the little bits of skin add color and texture). Both are available in most supermarkets and natural-food markets.

If you prefer, you can make almond flour or meal yourself by grinding either blanched slivered almonds or sliced almonds in a food processor or high-powered blender (such as Vitamix) until soft and powdery (see page 16). As a guide: 4¼ oz [120 g] almonds usually yields about 1 cup almond flour or meal.

BUTTER

Butter, butter, and more butter. I usually use unsalted butter for baking, adding the salt to my cake batters, fillings, and frostings myself. I always have salted butter on hand as well, for my morning slice of sourdough toast and the occasional batch of salted butter caramel sauce. When it comes to butter, you get what you pay for, so buy the best-quality butter you can afford. Sweet cream butter has a smooth,

neutral flavor and light texture that melts easily. Cultured European-style and Irish butters are created by adding live bacteria (cultures) to the cream before it is churned, giving it a slightly tangy flavor. Cultured butter also has a slightly higher milk-fat content than sweet cream butter, giving it a richer flavor and creamier texture. Some bakers feel the acidity in cultured butter gives cakes and other baked goods a more delicate and tender crumb.

Brown butter: When butter is melted and cooked until it begins to turn brown, it develops a sweet, nutty flavor and aroma as the milk solids caramelize. Brown butter, or *beurre noisette* in French, which literally translates to "hazelnut butter," is a delicious addition to cake batters, frostings, and buttercreams.

To make brown butter, in a saucepan over low heat, melt unsalted butter. When the butter is completely melted, increase the heat to medium-high and bring the butter to a boil. When butter boils, the hissing and burbling sounds like distant applause—this is the heat boiling away the water in the butter. When the sound fades, this means most of the water in the butter has been boiled away. Continue cooking, stirring constantly with a wooden spoon, until the milk solids at the bottom of the pan start to caramelize, turn brown, and develop a sweet, nutty aroma. The whole process will take 5 to 7 minutes. Remove the pan from the heat and immediately

pour the brown butter into a bowl. This will stop the cooking process and prevent the butter from becoming too dark or burning. Make sure to include all the nutty browned bits. Let cool. Brown butter can be refrigerated in a covered container for up to 1 week.

CHOCOLATE

I tested the recipes in this book with a variety of chocolates available in most standard grocery stores and large specialty markets, including Scharffen Berger, Lindt, Guittard, and Trader Joe's 72 percent dark chocolate bar. Callebaut and Valrhona are wonderful, if pricey, choices, and although not available in most grocery stores, they can be ordered online or from specialty baking shops and upscale markets. For more on chocolate, go to page 66.

CITRUS OILS

Lemon, orange, and lime oils add a serious punch of zesty, tangy flavor to cakes, frostings, and glazes. Citrus oils are cold-pressed from the rind of the fruit, and their flavor is concentrated and intense. Purchase the oils in small bottles, and refrigerate after opening. My favorite brand is Boyajian.

COCOA POWDER

There are two types of unsweetened cocoa powder—natural and Dutch-process. Dutch-process cocoa is the favorite of European bakers. Processed with alkali,

14

it is less acidic, richer, and darker in color than natural cocoa powder. For cakes leavened with baking powder alone, or in cakes leavened with beaten egg or egg whites and no chemical leavening, Dutch-process cocoa is the perfect choice. Natural cocoa powder is more common in American cake recipes that have a greater proportion of sugar, that include other acidic ingredients like buttermilk and sour cream, and are leavened with baking soda or a combination of baking powder and baking soda.

DULCE DE LECHE

Literally translated as "milk jam" or "milk sweet," dulce de leche is a delicately flavored milky caramel cream beloved throughout Latin America, where it is used to spread on toast, sandwich together buttery cookies called *alfajores*, or fill and frost cakes. If you don't want to make your own dulce de leche, look for the Argentinian brand La Salamandra, which is available from selected retailers and online. You can also try Nestlé brand La Lechera, which is widely available in most grocery stores and comes in both cans and bottles. Make sure to choose the canned version, as the bottled dulce de leche is more saucelike, and too thin for the recipes in this book. If these brands aren't available, choose one with a short ingredients list: milk, sugar, vanilla, and bicarbonate of soda. See "DIY Dulce de Leche," page 91, for a recipe to make at home.

EGGS

All the cakes in this book were tested with standard large eggs. Large eggs weigh about 55 g each.

Beating egg whites: To make the meringue frostings in this book, it's important to beat the egg whites into a stable foam. Follow these simple tips to get great results every time.

Separate eggs when they are cold, as they separate easily and cleanly that way. But for greater volume, let the egg whites come to room temperature before beating.

Keep egg whites fat-free. Egg whites must be free from any traces of yolk or other grease or oils to whip up properly. Any traces of fat will destroy the egg white's ability to trap and hold air. If you notice a touch of egg yolk in the separated whites, remove it with one of the empty egg shells; the yolk is drawn to the shell and will be easier to remove.

Use cream of tartar. Adding cream of tartar to the egg whites as you beat them will ensure that they develop a dense, creamy foam with maximum volume that is more stable and less likely to collapse.

Use a metal bowl. When beaten by hand, the classic choice is a copper bowl, but when using an electric mixer, beat the egg whites in a large stainless-steel bowl. It is difficult to remove all traces of oil and fat from plastic, and the smooth sides of glass or ceramic bowls make it hard for the whites to cling together and form a close, tight structure.

Start slowly for stability. To create a more stable foam with less chance of collapsing, start beating the whites at low speed, then increase the speed to medium-high when the whites are no longer viscous and just starting to foam. Starting at low speed will develop smaller bubbles that are inherently more stable than the large

bubbles that would form if you started beating the egg whites immediately at high speed.

Beat to soft peaks. Soft peaks could be described as soft, billowy mounds with well-defined peaks that slowly curve when the beaters are lifted. The beaten whites will not cling to the sides of the bowl, but rather will shift from side to side in one mass when the bowl is tilted. Egg whites beaten to the soft-peak stage are the perfect consistency for folding into cake batters. They are firm enough to hold their shape without deflating, but incorporate easily with the batter. Egg whites beaten to soft peaks will continue to expand in the oven when they are baked, ensuring high-rising cakes.

Beat to stiff, glossy peaks. Egg whites beaten to stiff, glossy peaks have a dense, creamy texture and stand firmly upright when the beaters are lifted. They are so firm that they will not fall out of the bowl if it is turned upside down. Until you can eyeball stiff peaks, feel free to stop the mixer and check how firmly the peaks stand up when the beaters are lifted.

Don't overbeat. After the egg whites have achieved stiff, glossy peaks, stop beating. Overbeating causes the whites to separate and become dry and granular, eventually collapsing.

Making meringue: Cakes iced with fluffy meringue frostings have a lusciously pretty, billowy allure. They are delicately flavored, with a marshmallow-y sweetness that melts in your mouth. I love meringue frostings slathered over vanilla cake layers filled with lemon curd, or showered with freshly grated coconut. Here are two of my favorite meringue frostings.

SEVEN-MINUTE FROSTING

This fluffy confection made from egg whites and sugar has been around for many years. The technique for preparing it is very similar to Swiss meringue. Both combine egg whites and sugar and beat them together over simmering water until the sugar dissolves and the mixture is light and frothy. Seven-Minute Frosting can get grainy if all the sugar isn't dissolved correctly. Beat everything but the vanilla together and test the temperature with a candy thermometer; it should read 120° to 140°F [50° to 60°C]—very hot to the touch. It's best served the day it is made.

1½ cups [300 g] sugar
2 Tbsp corn syrup
⅛ tsp salt
¼ cup [60 ml] water
2 egg whites
1½ tsp vanilla extract

Fill a 2- or 3-qt [2- or 2.8-L] saucepan one-third of the way with water. Bring to a boil over medium heat, uncovered.

In a 2½-qt [2.5-L] Pyrex or stainless-steel mixing bowl, combine the sugar, corn syrup, salt, water, and egg whites. With a hand mixer, beat for 1 minute on medium speed until combined and frothy. Place the bowl over the boiling water, making sure the water reaches up to just under the bottom of the bowl, but without touching it. Continue beating on high speed until light, fluffy, and thick enough to spread, 5 to 7 minutes. Beat in the vanilla. Use immediately.

WHITE MOUNTAIN FROSTING

This is very similar to Italian meringue: a hot sugar syrup is boiled to the soft-ball stage and then poured into egg whites beaten to soft peaks. The whites are then beaten again until stiff and glossy. A higher percentage of corn syrup prevents this frosting from getting grainy, so it will retain its marshmallow-y softness overnight.

4 egg whites
2 cups sugar
½ cup light corn syrup
⅓ cup water
2 tsp vanilla extract

In the bowl of a stand mixer fitted with the whisk attachment, beat the egg whites on high speed until they form soft peaks, 3 to 4 minutes.

While the egg whites are beating, combine the sugar, corn syrup, and water in a 3-qt [2.8-L] saucepan. Cover and bring to a rolling boil over medium-high heat. Uncover and boil gently for about 5 minutes without stirring, or until it reaches 240° to 242°F [115° to 116°C] on a candy thermometer. To accurately measure the temperature of the sugar syrup, tip the pan slightly so the syrup pools to one side and is deep enough for the thermometer to get a reading.

Continue beating the egg whites until they reach stiff peaks, a few minutes more. Pour the hot syrup in a steady stream into the egg whites, beating constantly on medium-high speed. Continue beating until the meringue is very white, fluffy, and glossy, about 10 minutes. Beat in the vanilla. Immediately spread over cake layers.

EXTRACTS AND FLAVORINGS

Always use extracts labeled "pure." Vanilla extracts can be blended or single origin. I always have bottles of Tahitian, Madagascar, and Mexican vanilla, as well as a bottle of blended extract, to choose from. See the facing page for more on vanilla extract and flavoring. It's a little harder to find pure coconut extract, so look for coconut flavoring (extracts are alcohol-based, whereas flavorings are oil-based) if you don't want to use imitation coconut extract.

FLOR DE JAMAICA

Also known as dried red hibiscus flowers, *flor de Jamaica* are used to make tea and to flavor sugar syrups. They are sold in bulk in most Latin American grocery stores, or can be found online.

FLOUR

For accuracy, I tested most of the cakes in this book with standard unbleached all-purpose flour (called "plain" flour in the U.K.) which has a 9 to 12 percent protein content. I also use cake flour, which is a lighter, finer-textured flour with a lower percentage of protein than all-purpose flour (about 7 to 8 percent protein). If cake flour isn't available, you can make your own version by substituting 1 cup [120 g] cake flour with ¾ cup [105 g] all-purpose flour sifted together with 2 tablespoons cornstarch (cornflour).

To accurately measure flour, stir the flour in the bag or canister to lighten, and spoon into the measuring cup, allowing it to overflow the top without tamping the flour down. With the back of a knife, scrape straight across the top of the cup, allowing the excess flour to fall back into the bag or canister.

FREEZE-DRIED FRUIT

Freeze-dried strawberries and raspberries, pineapple, mango, lychees, peaches, banana, and apples add an intense pop of fruit flavor to cakes without adding too much moisture. Freeze-dried fruit can be crushed into a fine powder and used alone, or in combination with fresh fruit, in batters and frostings. Crumbled freeze-dried fruit adds color, texture, and intense flavor when scattered like sprinkles on top of a frosted cake.

NUTS

For the freshest flavor, buy whole, shelled nuts (or shelled halves for walnuts and pecans). Whole, raw almonds and hazelnuts can be blanched or roasted and skinned as needed. Store nuts in the freezer, double-bagged in plastic freezer bags, to extend their shelf life and prevent them from going rancid. Nuts should be chopped first and then toasted to enhance their flavor.

Blanching pistachios: To unleash their vibrant green color, pistachios should be blanched before using in a recipe. In a large bowl, cover 1 cup shelled raw pistachios with about 2 in [5 cm] of boiling water. Let cool completely in the water, 20 to 30 minutes. Drain the nuts and place them on a clean kitchen towel. Cover with another towel and rub gently with your hands. As you do this, the friction will cause the loosened skins to come off. Spread the nuts in a single layer on a rimmed baking sheet and toast lightly in a preheated 300°F [150°C] oven for 15 minutes. Let cool completely before chopping.

Toasting nuts: To toast whole or chopped nuts, spread them in a single layer on a rimmed baking sheet and toast in a preheated 350°F [180°C] oven for 6 to 8 minutes, until warm and fragrant. Let cool completely before using.

Making nut flour: If you don't want to purchase almond or hazelnut meal, you can make your own. Combine 6 oz [170 g] skinned hazelnuts, or slivered or sliced almonds in a food processor fitted with the metal chopping blade. Using short pulses, grind the nuts until they are fine and powdery. If you like, you can also add 2 tablespoons of flour to the nuts before grinding them. The flour acts as a buffer; if ground alone, the nuts may become oily and pasty before they achieve the fine texture that's best for baking.

SALT

I use fine sea salt when I bake. It has a clean flavor that I like, without any chemical aftertaste, and it dissolves completely in most batters. It is easily accessible in most grocery stores and supermarkets. As a finishing salt to sprinkle over the top of a cake, or on candied nuts, I choose Maldon sea salt. It has a pleasing appearance; a delicate, crunchy texture, with flakes that crumble easily with your fingertips; and a fresh, lightly salty flavor.

SPIRITS AND BEER

If you like to drink spirits and beer, chances are you will like to bake with them, too. My favorite beers for baking are dark, malty milk stouts and refreshing hefeweizens that are brewed with spices and orange peel and sometimes flavored with honey. I always have bourbon, dark rum, Irish whiskey, and brandy for baking;

they're versatile and have a lot of flavor. For the coconut cakes, you can't beat a shot or two of Malibu coconut rum. For spirits I use less often, I look for small 50-ml bottles for single-use purposes.

SUGAR

I use pure cane sugar only. Like many pastry chefs, I think it simply works better, and though I can't scientifically prove it, I definitely feel it caramelizes better than sugar derived from sugar beets. Consider it my personal quirk. I use granulated sugar, golden and dark brown sugar, and confectioners' sugar in my recipes. In my pantry, I also have muscovado sugar, a natural brown sugar with a distinctive molasses flavor, and sparkly raw demerara and turbinado sugars. Superfine sugar, sometimes called "baker's sugar," is made especially for baking. It has an ultrafine grain that mixes, blends, and melts easily. You can duplicate this fine texture by grinding regular granulated sugar in a food processor, using the metal chopping blade, for about 1 minute, until the grains feel finer when rubbed between your fingers and thumb. Use as you would granulated sugar.

The best way to measure soft, moist brown sugar is to firmly pack it into a flat-edged, dry measuring cup. Use the back of a tablespoon to pack it into the cup. The brown sugar should hold the shape of the cup when it is turned out. I always measure confectioners' sugar first (unless a recipe specifically directs me to do otherwise), and then sift to remove any obvious lumps.

SYRUPS

Flavorful syrups add moisture and complexity to many cake batters, fruit compotes, glazes, and buttercreams. These are my favorites:

Maple syrup: The dark, deeply flavorful maple syrup once called "grade B" is now labeled "grade A: dark and robust." With its thicker texture and deep, rich, brown-sugary flavor, it is perfect for baking.

Golden syrup: This thick, amber-colored syrup has a buttery flavor. It is a by-product made when refining sugar cane juice into granulated sugar. I often use it instead of light corn syrup. Lyle's is the best-known brand.

Pomegranate molasses: Popular in the Middle East, pomegranate molasses is simply pomegranate juice that has been reduced down to an intense, sweet-and-sour syrup. It has the consistency of thick honey and adds a citrusy pop of flavor to glazes, frostings, and fruit compotes.

VANILLA

Every pastry chef worth her or his salt can wax poetic about the eternal allure of vanilla, but my favorite quote belongs to renowned pastry chef Gail Gand, who once called it "the underwear of baking." Vanilla is the invisible underpinning of so many great desserts, with its subtle but unmistakable perfume and compatibility with so many other flavors, from chocolate and caramel to coffee, banana, and warm spices like cinnamon, nutmeg, and cloves.

The vanilla bean is the cured seedpod of a climbing orchid native to Mexico. Second only to saffron in the effort and expense required to cultivate it, each orchid

blossom lasts only a single day before it falls from the vine, and must be pollinated by hand before it does so. Once pollinated, a single seedpod forms, which then takes 7 to 9 months to ripen. To become the dark, leathery bean we are familiar with, the seedpods endure a lengthy curing and drying process to develop their distinctive flavor and aroma.

Vanilla is cultivated in four major regions of the world, and each vanilla has its own unique flavor profile:

Indonesian: Smoky, with a slightly woody flavor, Indonesian vanilla beans are rarely used alone and are often combined with Madagascar beans for use in blended vanilla extracts.

Madagascar Bourbon: In the early 1800s, the French transplanted vanilla orchid cuttings from Mexico to Madagascar, one of the Bourbon Islands off the coast of Africa, for cultivation. Madagascar and the surrounding islands now produce the bulk of vanilla beans grown in the world. Buttery and sweet, Madagascar—or Bourbon—vanilla marries well with spirits like dark rum and whiskey and in buttery desserts, creamy puddings, and ice cream.

Mexican: Considered the birthplace of vanilla and the heart of vanilla bean cultivation for hundreds of years, Mexico's many vanilla plantations eventually dwindled in numbers as farmers turned to less time-consuming or more lucrative crops. Mexican vanilla beans are intense and rich, with a pungent, spicy flavor and aroma. They shine in recipes where vanilla is the star and not muted by other ingredients. A simple milkshake made with Mexican vanilla is a transcendent experience not to be missed.

Tahitian: Of all varieties of vanilla, Tahitian has the most delicate and fruity flavor, with a distinctive floral aroma. Ideal in fruit-based desserts from apples and pears to berries and stone fruits like cherries, apricots, and peaches, it is the perfect vanilla for flavoring Devonshire-Style Cream (page 163).

VANILLA FORMS

Vanilla beans: When buying vanilla beans, look for moist, supple pods that are plump and slightly sticky. This indicates how fresh and flavorful they are. Pods that are dry or hard have been stored improperly, are of poor quality, or are just old. To extract the thick, sticky seeds from inside the vanilla pod, split it in half lengthwise with a sharp paring knife. Scrape the seeds, or "caviar," from the pod using the back of the knife, sliding it down the length of the pod. Don't throw away the empty pod. Add it to a canister of sugar to make vanilla sugar, or to a pot of simmering milk or cream for use in puddings and pastry creams.

Beyond beans, you'll find vanilla at the store in two basic forms, vanilla bean paste and vanilla extract.

Vanilla bean paste: An alternative to using whole vanilla beans, paste is made from vanilla seeds preserved in a thick, sticky liquid. One tablespoon of vanilla paste equals the seeds of half a bean, or 1 teaspoon vanilla extract. Use vanilla bean paste in creams, puddings, and frostings where vanilla is the star, and the little black seeds will be visible.

Vanilla extract: Use only pure extracts made from real vanilla beans. Extract labeled simply as "pure vanilla" is usually made from a combination of beans from different regions. Alternatively, look for extracts made from single-origin beans from a specific location—usually Mexico, Madagascar, or Tahiti. Fine-quality vanilla extracts are available in single and double strength.

While visiting the Big Island in Hawaii, I toured the Hawaiian Vanilla Company, where many of the vanilla extracts are made using whiskey or dark rum, giving them an added level of complexity and flavor. Here is an easy recipe you can make at home.

HOMEMADE VANILLA BOURBON EXTRACT

2 cups [480 ml] bourbon or dark rum
1 Tbsp sugar
12 vanilla beans

Pour the bourbon into a 1-pint [480-ml] jar with a tight-fitting screw-top lid. Stir in the sugar. Split each vanilla bean in half lengthwise and scrape the seeds into the liquor. Cover the jar and shake gently to agitate and distribute the seeds throughout the liquor. Uncover and add the scraped pods to the jar, making sure the pods are completely submerged. Cover tightly and store in a cool, dry place to age, about 2 to 4 months. The vanilla will keep indefinitely.

VEGETABLE SHORTENING

I prefer to use shortening or nonstick cooking spray to grease cake pans. Butter isn't a solid fat and contains a little water, so using it can lead to sticking when it melts as the batter bakes.

BUILDING A BETTER CAKE

Butter, sugar, eggs, flour, and milk are simple ingredients which, when properly combined, are transformed into a tender, beautiful cake—you just need to know how to put them all together to make some magic.

PREP THE CAKE PANS

The few minutes needed to prepare your cake pan(s) properly is time well spent.

To keep cakes from sticking, coat the bottom and sides of the pan(s) with nonstick cooking spray or a nonstick baking spray with added flour. If you don't want to use a nonstick spray, brush the pan with solid vegetable shortening or vegetable oil (do not use butter—it sticks) and sprinkle the pan with 1 to 2 Tbsp flour. Lift the pan and tilt it, shaking it slightly to distribute the flour onto all the greased surfaces. Shake out any excess flour.

Line the bottom of the pan with parchment paper. Parchment paper rounds are available in all pan sizes, or you can buy parchment paper by the roll and simply trace the bottom of the pan on the parchment paper using a pencil, then cut it out (inside the pencil marks).

CREAM THE BUTTER AND SUGAR

Creating light, tender, fine-grained butter cakes starts with creaming together room temperature butter and sugar by beating with an electric mixer. The tiny, sharp crystals in the sugar bite into the softened butter, creating little bubbles of air, the first step in the leavening process.

The addition of eggs and chemical leavening agents like baking powder and baking soda enlarge the little air bubbles created in the batter through creaming, and help the cake to rise in the oven. Proper creaming promises a silky texture and a delicate crumb.

The room-temperature butter (65° to 70°F [18° to 21°C]) should be soft enough to hold a deep fingerprint when pressed, but not so soft that it starts to slump over and look oily. Beat the butter alone on low speed to lighten it, then add the sugar gradually. As the sugar crystals cut into the butter, small air pockets form, increasing the volume of the mixture.

Beat the butter and sugar together for 3 to 5 minutes at medium-high speed; the mixture will become a pale, creamy yellow and increase in volume. When the sugar crystals are barely visible and the mixture is fluffy, you will know you've got it right.

ADD THE EGGS

Have you ever wondered why your cake recipes require the eggs to be at room temperature before you start? If cold eggs are added to the creamed butter and sugar, tiny little bits of the butter will seize and harden slightly, making it harder to smoothly incorporate the eggs, and inhibiting the batter's ability to rise as well as it should. Take the eggs from the refrigerator about an hour or two before you start to make your cake. You can speed up the process by sitting the eggs (in their shells) in a bowl of very warm water for about 10 minutes.

Separating eggs is easier to manage when the eggs are cold: Quickly crack the eggs on the rim of a bowl or cup and insert a thumb into either side of the crack. Separate the shell into two pieces, allowing the white to drip into the bowl as you transfer the yolk to one side of the shell. When the white is completely separated, drop the yolk into a separate bowl. Store the yolks in one bowl and the whites in another, allowing them to come to room temperature before using.

SIFT THE DRY INGREDIENTS

To sift or not to sift? That is the question. The dry ingredients, including the flour(s), salt, leavening agents, and spices can be combined in a small bowl and simply whisked together to blend them before adding to the batter, but I still believe in sifting. I don't use a sifter, just a fine-mesh sieve. Sifting breaks up any lumps in the flour or leavening agents and ensures that they are incorporated evenly in the batter. Flour is usually sifted after it is measured, although in some isolated cases, as in the

Hot Milk Sponge Cake for the Pastel de Tres Leches (page 100), the flour is sifted and then measured, and then sifted a few more times before it is incorporated with the remaining ingredients. Sifting aerates the dry ingredients, which yields a lighter, fluffier cake.

FOLD EVERYTHING TOGETHER

In a classic butter cake, the dry ingredients and wet ingredients are added to the creamed butter-sugar-egg mixture in stages, alternating between the two until the batter is smooth. This is where things get tricky; the proteins in the flour form gluten when combined with the water, coffee, milk, cream, or whatever liquid you are using. The more you mix the batter, the more gluten is developed (great in bread, not so great in cake). Too much gluten equals a tough cake. You need to alternate adding the dry and liquid ingredients, and fold them in gently. If you use an electric mixer, it only takes a few seconds to beat each addition into the batter. If overworked, your cake will rise poorly and have the texture of a hockey puck, so be gentle.

Folding fluffy ingredients like whipped cream and meringue into your batters properly is crucial for ensuring a light, airy texture. Here are some tips.

The Tool: Use a large, flat, heatproof rubber or silicone spatula to fold the ingredients together.

The Technique: When folding beaten egg whites into a heavier base, make sure to add the whites to the batter, and not the other way around—pouring a heavy batter over the delicate, whipped egg whites will deflate them, and the cake will not rise properly.

Up and Over: With the spatula, cut straight down into the center of the bowl, scooping the mixture up from the bottom and lifting it over the top of the batter. Give the bowl a half turn and continue folding the mixture up and over itself to incorporate the ingredients together.

Enough Is Enough: It's important to know when to stop folding, to avoid deflating the mixture. Every last speck of egg white or whipped cream doesn't need to disappear completely—err on the side of caution to avoid deflating your batter.

BAKE TO PERFECTION

Preheat your oven for about 15 minutes to make sure it has reached the optimum temperature. Use an oven thermometer to double-check that your oven is reaching the correct temperature. Bake the cake on the center rack in the oven and start checking for doneness about three-fourths of the way through the baking time. Don't open the oven door too soon, or the cake might collapse. Most recipes, the ones in this book included, give a range of cooking times to compensate for the temperature differences between ovens. Start checking the cake at the minimum baking time, but use all of your senses—including your common sense—to tell when it is done. You will know the cake is close to being done when you start to smell it. When you take a peek in the oven, the cake will have risen and lost its glossy appearance. Next, the cake will start to brown, and may start to pull away from the sides of the pan, but not always. If it's brown around the edges but still soft or wobbly in the middle, it needs more time in the oven. The best tool to test for doneness is a wooden skewer. I like using a wooden skewer instead of a toothpick because there is more surface area and you can easily see if any uncooked batter or stray crumbs are clinging to it.

COOL IT

When done, transfer the cake pans to a wire rack to cool. Cakes need to cool in their pans for a few minutes before unmolding. This gives the cake time to settle and firm up a bit. A 10-minute rest will prevent the cake from cracking or falling apart once it's turned out of the pan. If you have greased the pan well and lined it with parchment paper, the cake will pop out easily. Make sure to let the cake layers cool completely before you frost them. The only exception to this rule is if you are using a syrup to flavor and moisten the cake; if that is the case, brush the warm syrup on the cake while it, too, is still warm, ensuring that it will absorb the syrup completely.

STORING AND FREEZING CAKE LAYERS

When you're creating a complicated layer cake with many components, breaking the work up over a series of days makes the job easier and less stressful. Making the cake layers ahead of time and freezing them until you need them is one way to do this.

After baking the cake layers, transfer each completely cooled, unfrosted cake layer to a cardboard cake round and wrap tightly in two layers of plastic wrap, then in aluminum foil, and freeze for up to 2 weeks. Up to 15 hours before serving, remove the foil but not the plastic wrap from the cake layers and thaw at room temperature. When completely thawed, unwrap the layers and fill, stack, and frost the cake.

A BEAUTIFUL FINISH

You've baked and cooled your cake layers; now it's time to fill, stack, and frost them.

SPLITTING THE CAKE LAYERS

There are lots of complicated methods for splitting one cake layer into two equal layers, involving rulers and toothpicks and dental floss or cake-splitting tools that you can't fit in your tool drawer. But the fastest and easiest (and laziest) method I know, and the one I turn to time and time again, involves one simple trick that will ensure that your cake won't be lopsided, even if you don't split your cake layers with the same precision required to split the atom.

Start with cold cake layers. If just baked, let the cake layers cool completely, wrap in plastic wrap, and freeze for 15 to 20 minutes. (Alternatively, you can refrigerate the cake layers overnight.) Cold cake layers are firmer and less likely to crumble or tear when you split them.

Place the first cake layer, bottom-side up, on a cardboard cake round. This gives the cake a nice flat surface for frosting, and eliminates the need to cut away any cake to make it level.

With a paring knife, cut a tiny (approximately ¼-in [6-mm]) triangular-shaped notch out of the side of the cake—big enough to see, but small enough to be hidden easily when the cake is frosted.

Place the cake layer on a turntable. With the paring knife, score a line halfway up the side of the cake and all the way around, to act as a guide when you begin cutting the cake in half horizontally. Place one hand on top of the cake to steady it and with the other hand, using a long serrated knife, begin slicing through the cake with a gentle sawing motion, following the line you scored into the cake, to form two even layers.

Slip a second cardboard cake round (or the bottom of a removable tart pan) between the sliced layers. Remove the top layer and set aside.

Once you have spread the bottom layer with frosting or other filling, replace the top cake layer, carefully settling it over the filling and lining up the triangular notches to ensure the cake is level.

FILLING THE CAKE

Cake layers can be filled with jam, pudding, fresh fruit and pastry cream or citrus curds, thick caramel, or simply with the same frosting or buttercream used to frost the exterior of the cake. If you are using a soft filling like whipped cream, jam, citrus curds, or pudding, a few extra steps are needed to prevent the filling from bulging or oozing out from between the layers after the cake is frosted. To prevent this from happening, build a buttercream dam to hold in your filling:

1. Place the first cake layer, bottom-side up, on a cardboard cake round.

2. Fit a disposable piping bag with a large round decorating tip and fill it with about 1 to 2 cups of dense, firm frosting or buttercream. Use the same frosting or buttercream that you will use to frost the outside of the cake.

3. Pipe a thick rope of the buttercream on top of the cake layer, about ¼ inch from the edge, to form a circular dam.

4. Spread your filling in an even layer inside the buttercream dam, making sure that the filling does not rise above the dam. Gently top with a cake second layer bottom-side down (or if this is a split layer, line up the notches to make sure the layers are even; see "Splitting the Cake Layers," left).

5. Continue filling and stacking your cake layers. When complete, refrigerate for 15 to 30 minutes to allow the layers to set before continuing to frost the outside of the cake.

FROSTING THE CAKE

This can be a daunting process for many bakers, who long for a perfectly smooth finish but aren't sure how to achieve it. Professional pastry chefs know the secret to a beautifully frosted cake is to start with a "crumb coat."

The crumb coat: A crumb coat is a very thin layer of frosting covering the top and sides of the stacked layer cake. It acts as a base coat to seal in any errant crumbs. It's like a primer or spackle for your cake, sealing in the pores and imperfections, giving you a smooth canvas to apply the final beauty coat of buttercream.

Once the cake is filled and stacked, drop a large dollop of soft frosting or buttercream on top of the cake. Use an offset spatula to spread the frosting in a very thin layer over the top, pushing it over the edges of the cake. Pull the excess buttercream around the sides of the cake, filling in any nooks and crannies for a smooth, even coat. Keep spreading and smoothing the buttercream around the cake, making sure to keep the spatula on the frosting at all times, as you pull it over the unfrosted portions of the cake—this will prevent more crumbs from mixing in with this initial coat.

Once the top and sides of the cake are completely covered in frosting, smooth the top of the crumb coat with a long offset spatula or bench scraper, and then tidy the sides by holding the blade firmly against the cake and scraping it evenly all the way around the sides of the cake for a smooth finish. (A turntable works beautifully here: slowly spin the turntable while holding the offset spatula or bench scraper against the cake.) Refrigerate the crumb-coated cake for at least 30 minutes (and up to overnight, if you need to) allowing it to set before adding the final coat of buttercream.

The final coat: If the crumb coat is properly chilled and firm, the soft, room-temperature buttercream should glide smoothly and easily over the surface for a perfect finish. Start with a large dollop of buttercream on top of the cake. Spread and smooth it back and forth over the top and around the sides of the cake, making sure that the spatula stays on the frosting at all times as you work.

With this final coat of buttercream, you can go for an old-fashioned look and cover the cake in thick swirls of frosting, or give the cake a smooth, clean-lined look: Using a long offset spatula or bench scraper, and holding it firmly against the cake at an angle, pull the blade evenly around the sides of the cake for a smooth finish (again, a turntable is very handy here). Finally, smooth the top of the cake, pulling any excess buttercream from around the edges and smoothing it towards the center of the cake for a flat, even finish.

BUTTERCREAM BOOT CAMP

There are icings, there are frostings, and then there are The Buttercreams. These latter are frothy, mousselike amalgamations of eggs and sugar and lots and lots of butter. They may seem a little intimidating and labor-intensive at first, but oh-so-worth it once you take that first silky, sweet bite. Heaven.

A confession, before you start: You really need a stand mixer to master these classic buttercreams—the time required to beat them is formidable.

SWISS MERINGUE BUTTERCREAM

Sturdy, yet remarkably silky and creamy, this is the easiest of all the classic buttercreams to master. Egg whites and sugar are whisked together by hand in the bowl of a stand mixer set over simmering water until the sugar dissolves and the egg whites are warm and frothy. The bowl of frothy egg whites is transferred to the stand mixture and beaten into a stiff, glossy meringue. With the mixer running, softened butter is added, a little at a time, until the meringue is transformed into a smooth, creamy buttercream.

ITALIAN MERINGUE BUTTERCREAM

Despite its more delicate texture, Italian meringue buttercream is actually more durable than its Swiss cousin. Hot sugar syrup is poured in a steady stream into softly beaten egg whites, then beaten again to stiff, glossy peaks. As with the Swiss meringue, the butter is beaten in, a little at a time, until the buttercream is glossy and creamy.

FRENCH MERINGUE BUTTERCREAM

Meet the most challenging of all the egg-based buttercreams to master. This ultra-rich frosting is similar to Italian buttercream, but involves beating hot sugar syrup into egg yolks instead of egg whites until they are thick and lemon colored. Soft butter is beaten in a little at a time until the buttercream is smooth and velvety.

GERMAN BUTTERCREAM

Creamier and more robust than Swiss, Italian, and French versions, German buttercream, or *crème mousseline* in French, is basically pudding (or pastry cream) with lots of butter beaten into it. Think of it as buttercream that's just eaten a really big dinner; it's dense and velvety and supremely delicious.

"GOLDILOCKS" BUTTERCREAM

My favorite of all the egg-based buttercreams, this version is a bit of a mash-up of the Swiss and French meringue methods. I bypass the sugar syrup completely and beat whole eggs and granulated sugar together by hand in the bowl of a stand mixer over simmering water, beating until the sugar is dissolved and the eggs are thick and frothy, with a soft, mousselike consistency. Off the heat, the eggs are beaten on high speed using a stand mixer and whisk attachment until they triple in volume and the bowl is completely cool. Next, the softened butter is beaten in, a little at a time, just as with the Swiss, Italian, or French buttercreams. "Goldilocks" is easier to make than French buttercream, but it's creamier and has more heft and body than Swiss or Italian buttercream—yes, I will say it: It's just right.

SWEET AND EASY FROSTINGS TO LOVE

Although the terms "icing" and "frosting" are often used interchangeably, I always think of an icing as lighter and thinner, more like a glaze, and frosting as the thicker, richer, butterier concoction used to slather over layer cakes. When you are looking for a frosting that is a little less complicated than a classic meringue buttercream, these sweet options are easy to prepare.

ERMINE FROSTING

Sometimes called roux-, flour-, or boiled-milk buttercream, this silky frosting starts with a thick pudding-like base made from flour, sugar, and milk or light cream. The first time you make it, there will likely come a point when you start to doubt its success—but take heart! The final frosting has a light, velvety texture and mellow sweetness. As a bonus, it is very easy to make. Once the pudding base has cooled completely, butter is beaten in, 1 or 2 Tbsp at a time, until thick and creamy. Use the frosting as soon as you make it, or let it sit at room temperature for a few hours until you are ready to use it. Do not refrigerate the frosting before you need it to frost your cake, as it tends to lose its creamy texture, break, or look curdled when it returns to room temperature and you begin to spread it over your cake. This frosting is used in the Tennessee Whiskey Pecan Cake on page 148.

CREAM-CHEESE FROSTING

No carrot cake would be the same without it. Butter and cream cheese are beaten together with just enough confectioners' sugar to make a sweet and spreadable frosting. Blend in brown butter (see page 13) and vanilla bean paste for added complexity, or beat in finely crushed freeze-dried fruit and a little fresh fruit purée for an extra burst of flavor and color. The Chubby Bunny cake on page 166 features this frosting.

BUTTER FROSTING

Sometimes called "American Buttercream," this is the easiest frosting of all—simply beat butter and confectioners' sugar together until creamy, add a splash of milk or cream, and beat until spreadable.

There is a dispute among biblical scholars over which fruit Eve actually enticed Adam with in that idyllic garden so long ago. Although the apple has garnered all the press, others have insisted on the pomegranate or the fig. But the latest contender in the great debate is the banana. And if that historical tidbit doesn't tickle your inner stand-up comedian, I don't know what will.

Bananas are indeed a temptation. Their flavor and aroma are lush and tropical yet endearingly familiar, as we add them to our morning smoothies and school lunch boxes every day. But every good baker knows, whether it's drenched in caramel, layered with chocolate and buttercream, or just stirred into a simple golden loaf, where the banana really shines and reaches true glory is in a good banana cake. That's one temptation no one can resist.

BANANA BASICS

I always have a bunch of bananas on my kitchen counter. No matter their stage of ripeness, I can always find a way to use them. For snacking, I like bananas when they are barely ripe, firm to the touch, and bright yellow. The next day, when their color has deepened and their texture has grown a little softer, I'll add them to my breakfast fruit smoothie. If I am feeling extravagant, I'll make Bananas Foster, simmering thick slices of barely ripe banana in a bath of melted butter, brown sugar, cinnamon, and a splash of dark rum to spoon over ice cream.

The perfect banana for baking takes a little more time; when it's decidedly overripe and beyond consideration for eating out of hand, and its yellow jacket is heavily freckled and streaked with brown, that is when a banana is perfect for baking. It should be soft and tender, giving way without a whisper of resistance under the gentle pressure of a fork. Don't be tempted to use rougher methods on your bananas—a fork will transform the banana into a thick, chunky purée. You want to retain a bit of texture; if it is puréed down to a mush, it will become too liquid and upset the balance of ingredients in your cake batter.

Bananas taste best when left to ripen naturally on their own, developing a rich, sweet flavor and heady aroma—but in a pinch, place your bananas in a brown bag and seal to speed up ripening. You can also place barely ripe (yellow with no hints of green), unpeeled bananas on a parchment paper–lined baking sheet and cook them in a 300°F [150°C] oven for about 30 minutes, until they are very soft and the skins are deeply brown, almost black. This method is good in a pinch, as it softens the bananas and brings out the fruits' sugar.

I usually have an abundance of ripe bananas, but on one occasion when a banana birthday cake was required, I found myself in possession of a surly bunch that refused to ripen on time. Rather than baking the bananas in their skins, I peeled, sliced, and sautéed them in a little butter and brown sugar à la Bananas Foster before crushing them into a purée. Cooking softened the fruits' texture, unleashing the unmistakable banana fragrance and flavor, and the cake was just as delicious as it would have been with naturally ripened bananas.

Some might call this banana bread, but who are we kidding? It's really just naked cake, with the pure, sweet flavor of ripe banana. The combination of oil and melted butter gives this easy loaf a particularly velvety crumb. Make sure your bananas are deeply ripe and fragrant, dark yellow, and heavily freckled and streaked with brown, but not so dark that the fruit has started to ferment. If you want, you can add a handful of chopped toasted pecans or walnuts to the batter, and drizzle the cooled cake with a simple maple glaze.

BANANA-BUTTERSCOTCH LOAF

SERVES **6** TO **8**

1¾ cups [245 g] all-purpose flour

1 tsp baking powder

½ tsp baking soda

¾ tsp fine sea salt

½ tsp freshly grated nutmeg

2 eggs

1 cup [200 g] granulated sugar

¾ cup [150 g] firmly packed dark brown sugar

1 cup [230 g] mashed overripe bananas

½ cup [120 ml] vegetable oil

4 Tbsp [55 g] unsalted butter, melted

1½ tsp vanilla extract

MAPLE GLAZE

½ cup [60 g] confectioners' sugar

1 Tbsp maple syrup

¼ tsp vanilla extract

1 to 2 Tbsp milk

Position a rack in the center of the oven. Preheat the oven to 350°F [180°C]. Coat a 9-by-5-in [23-by-12-cm] metal loaf pan lightly with nonstick cooking spray. Line the pan with an 8½-by-15-in [21.5-by-38-cm] strip of parchment paper so it covers the bottom of the pan and hangs over the long sides.

In a medium bowl, sift together the flour, baking powder, baking soda, salt, and nutmeg.

In a separate medium bowl, whisk together the eggs, granulated sugar, brown sugar, bananas, oil, melted butter, and vanilla until smooth.

Gently fold the wet ingredients into the dry ingredients using a rubber or silicone spatula or wire whisk, just until the batter is smooth. Scrape the batter into the prepared pan and spread evenly with the spatula.

Bake for 55 to 60 minutes, until a wooden skewer inserted into the center of the cake comes out clean.

Transfer the pan to a wire rack and let cool for 10 minutes. Then, grasping the overhanging parchment, lift the loaf out of the pan and set it on the cooling rack. Let cool completely. Discard the parchment paper.

TO MAKE THE GLAZE: While the cake is cooling, in a bowl, whisk together the confectioners' sugar, maple syrup, vanilla, and just enough of the milk to make a thick, pourable glaze. Drizzle the glaze over the top of the cake. Let cool completely before slicing and serving.

Store the cake at room temperature, wrapped well, for up to 3 days.

This little tea cake appears so simple, so unassuming. In a cake beauty pageant, she's just the plain little girl next door. But plumb her depths, and she has a dark, rich, seductive secret. A thin ribbon of dense, fudgy brownie is swirled into the center of this everyday banana cake, and it comes as a sweet surprise when you slice it. Irresistible.

BANANA-BROWNIE SWIRL CAKE

SERVES 6 TO 8

BROWNIE BATTER
5 Tbsp unsalted butter

1 oz [30 g] unsweetened chocolate, coarsely chopped

½ cup [100 g] sugar

1 egg, at room temperature

1 tsp vanilla extract

4 Tbsp all-purpose flour

⅛ tsp fine sea salt

BANANA BATTER
½ cup [110 g] unsalted butter, at room temperature

1 cup [200 g] sugar

2 eggs, at room temperature

1 tsp vanilla extract

1 cup [230 g] mashed overripe bananas

¼ cup [60 ml] buttermilk

1½ cups [210 g] all-purpose flour

1 tsp baking powder

¼ tsp baking soda

½ tsp fine sea salt

Position a rack in the center of the oven. Preheat the oven to 350°F [180°C]. Coat a 9-by-5-in [23-by-12-cm] metal loaf pan with nonstick cooking spray. Line the pan with an 8½-by-15-in [21.5-by-38-cm] strip of parchment paper so it covers the bottom of the pan and hangs over the long sides.

TO MAKE THE BROWNIE BATTER: In a microwave-safe bowl, microwave the butter and chocolate together on high for 1 minute. Stir until completely melted. Stir the sugar, egg, and vanilla into the chocolate mixture. Add the flour and salt and mix just until smooth. Set aside to cool slightly.

TO MAKE THE BANANA BATTER: In a large bowl, with an electric mixer set on medium speed, beat together the butter and sugar until light and fluffy, 3 to 4 minutes. Scrape down the sides of the bowl and beat in the eggs, one at a time, and then beat in the vanilla, bananas, and buttermilk. Sift the flour, baking powder, baking soda, and salt over the banana batter. Fold together by hand using a rubber or silicone spatula, just until smooth.

Spoon half of the banana batter into the prepared loaf pan and spread evenly with the spatula. Spread the brownie batter over the banana batter in an even layer. Scrape the remaining banana batter over the brownie batter, smoothing evenly.

Bake for 45 to 55 minutes, until the cake is firm and golden brown and a wooden skewer inserted into the center comes out clean or with just a few moist crumbs clinging to it.

Transfer the pan to a wire rack and let cool for 10 minutes. Then, grasping the overhanging parchment, lift the loaf out of the pan and set it on the cooling rack. Discard the parchment paper. In order to preserve an attractive ripple in the center, let the cake cool completely at room temperature for at least a few hours, but preferably overnight, before slicing. This gives the brownie layer a chance to completely solidify, and for the flavors to ripen. Cut into slices and serve, or wrap well in plastic wrap and store at room temperature for up to 3 days.

Although it feels like a vintage cake, hummingbird cake is actually a relatively new Southern classic, created in the late 1970s by a home baker from North Carolina. The original recipe combined cubed bananas, canned crushed pineapple, and pecans in a simple cinnamon-spiced cake iced with a rich cream-cheese frosting. I've updated the recipe into a simple breakfast cake, folding chunks of fresh pineapple and flaked coconut into a banana cake batter, and sprinkling the top with sparkling demerara sugar and chunks of toasted pecans. Look for peeled fresh pineapple spears in the refrigerated section of the produce aisle to save time.

HUMMINGBIRD MORNING CAKE

SERVES 9

2 cups [240 g] cake flour

1 tsp baking powder

½ tsp baking soda

1 tsp fine sea salt

1¼ tsp ground cinnamon

¼ tsp freshly grated nutmeg

1½ cups [180 g] pecan halves, toasted
(see page 16)

¾ cup [165 g] unsalted butter, at room
temperature

1 cup [200 g] granulated sugar

½ cup [100 g] firmly packed dark brown sugar

2 eggs, at room temperature

1 tsp vanilla extract

1 cup [230 g] mashed overripe bananas

¼ cup [60 ml] buttermilk

1 cup [60 g] sweetened, flaked coconut

8 oz [230 g] fresh ripe pineapple,
very finely chopped

3 Tbsp demerara sugar or raw sugar

Position a rack in the center of the oven. Preheat the oven to 350°F [180°C]. Coat the bottom and sides of a 9-in [23-cm] square baking pan with nonstick cooking spray, and line the bottom with parchment paper.

In a medium bowl, sift together the cake flour, baking powder, baking soda, salt, cinnamon, and nutmeg; set aside. Coarsely chop 1 cup [120 g] of the pecans; set aside.

In a separate medium bowl, with an electric mixer set on medium speed, beat together the butter, granulated sugar, and brown sugar until light and fluffy, 4 to 5 minutes. Scrape down the sides of the bowl and beat in the eggs, one at a time, and then beat in the vanilla, bananas, and buttermilk, just until combined. With the mixer set at low speed, beat the flour mixture into the banana batter, in two additions, just until combined. With a rubber spatula, fold in the 1 cup chopped pecans with the coconut and the pineapple.

Scrape the batter into the prepared pan and spread evenly with the spatula. Sprinkle with the remaining ½ cup [60 g] pecan halves and the demerara sugar.

Bake for 45 to 50 minutes, until the cake is firm and golden brown and a wooden skewer inserted into the center comes out clean.

Transfer the pan to a wire rack and let cool for 15 minutes. Invert the cake onto the rack and discard the parchment paper. Invert the cake again, onto a serving plate or cake stand, with the sugary nut side up. Cut into squares and serve, or wrap well in plastic wrap and store at room temperature for up to 3 days.

"Whoa, Nelly!" I can hear you say. "Do I really need that much frosting?" There is enough here to frost either a double or triple layer cake, and I find it's always better to have too much rather than too little frosting. In a word: spackle! If you aren't used to frosting layer cakes, a little extra frosting can be your best friend, as it covers a multitude of sins. The good news is, any leftover frosting can be squirreled away in the fridge to spread on graham crackers as a well-deserved treat later on. The addition of brown butter in the cake and in the frosting adds an extra nuance of flavor. Called *beurre noisette* by the French, for the nutty aroma it develops as the butterfat melts and the milk solids caramelize, brown butter adds complexity, intensifying the flavor of the banana in the cake layers while it tempers the sweetness of the frosting.

BROWN-BUTTER BANANA CAKE
WITH BROWN-BUTTER CREAM-CHEESE FROSTING

SERVES 8 TO 10

1½ cups [330 g] unsalted butter
3 cups [420 g] all-purpose flour
2 tsp baking powder
1 tsp baking soda
1 tsp fine sea salt
4 eggs, at room temperature
1½ cups [300 g] firmly packed dark brown sugar
1¼ cups [250 g] granulated sugar
2 cups [460 g] mashed overripe bananas
¾ cup [180 g] sour cream
2 tsp vanilla extract
3 Tbsp dark rum or bourbon

BROWN-BUTTER CREAM-CHEESE FROSTING
1 cup [220 g] unsalted butter
1 lb [455 g] cream cheese, at room temperature
1 Tbsp vanilla bean paste
1 teaspoon vanilla extract
2 Tbsp dark rum
⅛ tsp fine sea salt
6 to 8 cups [720 to 960 g] confectioners' sugar

CROWD-PLEASER

Position a rack in the center of the oven. Preheat the oven to 350°F [180°C]. Coat two or three 9-in [23-cm] round cake pans with nonstick cooking spray and line the bottoms with parchment paper.

In a medium saucepan over low heat, melt the butter. When the butter is completely melted, increase the heat to high and bring the butter to a boil. Continue cooking, stirring often with a wooden spoon, until the milk solids at the bottom of the pan begin to brown. The butter will develop a sweet, nutty aroma—this should take 5 to 7 minutes. Immediately pour the butter into a bowl to cool and prevent it from cooking any further, making sure to scrape in all the tasty browned bits. Set aside.

Sift the flour, baking powder, baking soda, and salt into a medium bowl. Set aside.

In a large bowl with an electric mixer (or a stand mixer fitted with the whisk attachment) set on medium-high speed, beat the eggs until frothy. Gradually add the brown sugar and granulated sugar and

Continued

continue beating until thick and fluffy and doubled in volume, 3 to 4 minutes. Beat in the bananas, sour cream, vanilla, and rum. Add the dry ingredients to the batter in two additions, beating on low speed just until combined, 10 to 15 seconds after each addition. Fold the brown butter into the batter by hand, using a rubber or silicone spatula, just until smooth. Divide the batter evenly between the prepared cake pans, smoothing the tops with the spatula.

Bake for 35 to 40 minutes (for two 9-inch layers) or 25 to 30 minutes (for three 9-inch layers), until the cake is golden brown and a wooden skewer inserted into the center comes out clean.

Transfer the pans to wire racks and let cool for 10 minutes. Invert the cake layers onto the racks to finish cooling, and discard the parchment paper.

TO MAKE THE FROSTING: In a medium saucepan over low heat, melt the butter. When the butter is completely melted, increase the heat to high and bring the butter to a boil. Continue cooking, stirring often, until the milk solids at the bottom of the pan begin to brown. The butter will develop a sweet, nutty aroma—this should take 5 to 7 minutes. Immediately pour the butter into a bowl to cool and prevent the butter from cooking any further, making sure to include all the delicious browned bits. Cover and refrigerate the butter until firm, 20 to 30 minutes.

Combine the cream cheese and chilled brown butter in a stand mixer fitted with the paddle attachment. Beat on low speed until smooth and creamy, about 1 minute. Beat in the vanilla bean paste and vanilla extract, the salt, and 4 cups [480 g] of the confectioners' sugar until smooth. Beat in the rum. At this point, the frosting should be thick but spreadable. If it is too thin, beat in as much of the remaining 2 to 4 cups [240 to 480 g] confectioners' sugar as needed to reach the desired consistency. Set aside.

TO FINISH THE CAKE: Place the first cake layer, bottom-side up, on a cardboard cake round, or directly on a cake plate or cake stand. Top with about one-third of the frosting, or one-fourth of the frosting if you are building a triple layer cake, spreading it in an even layer to the edge of the cake. Top with the second cake layer. Repeat to fill and frost a third cake layer, if using. Refrigerate the stacked cake layers for 30 minutes to firm up. Apply a very thin layer of frosting over the top and around the sides of the cake to create a crumb coat (see page 21). Refrigerate the cake for 15 to 20 minutes to set the crumb coat. Spread the remaining frosting evenly over the top and sides of the cake. Serve immediately, or refrigerate the cake in a covered cake carrier for up to 2 days, allowing the cake to come to room temperature for 1 or 2 hours before slicing.

Shirley Corriher, author of the indispensable *BakeWise*, likes to fold a little whipped heavy cream into her cake batter right before baking. This technique gives her cakes a suave, velvety texture, and I love doing the same in this banana cake. The layers are rich, but so tender and light that even drenched in dulce de leche and piled high with sliced bananas and mounds of whipped cream, this cake feels fresher and more delicate than a traditionally frosted cake—the perfect choice for people who aren't as fond of buttercream as I am.

BANANALICIOUS

SERVES 8 TO 10

3 cups [420 g] all-purpose flour

2 tsp baking powder

1 tsp baking soda

1¼ tsp fine sea salt

1 tsp cinnamon

½ tsp freshly grated nutmeg

1½ cups [345 g] mashed overripe bananas

4 eggs

1½ cups [300 g] granulated sugar

1 cup [200 g] firmly packed dark brown sugar

½ cup [110 g] unsalted butter, melted

½ cup [120 ml] coconut oil, melted, or canola oil

⅔ cup [160 ml] buttermilk

2 tsp vanilla extract

½ cup [120 ml] heavy cream

TO FINISH

3 cups [720 ml] cold heavy cream

1½ cups [345 g] plus 2¼ cups [520 g] dulce de leche, store-bought or DIY (page 91)

2 tsp vanilla bean paste

1 tsp vanilla extract

2 Tbsp dark rum

3 to 4 large barely ripe bananas, sliced ½ in [12 mm] thick

Position a rack in the center of the oven. Preheat the oven to 350°F [180°C]. Coat three 8-in [20-cm] or 9-in [23-cm] round cake pans with nonstick cooking spray and line the bottoms with parchment paper.

In a large bowl, sift together the flour, baking powder, baking soda, salt, cinnamon, and nutmeg.

In a separate large bowl, whisk together the mashed bananas, eggs, granulated sugar, brown sugar, melted butter, melted coconut oil, buttermilk, and vanilla.

Make a well in the middle of the dry ingredients. Pour in the wet ingredients and gently whisk the two together just until smooth. In a medium bowl, beat the heavy cream on medium-low speed with an electric hand mixer until it forms soft peaks. With a flat rubber or silicone spatula, gently fold the whipped cream into the batter. Divide the batter between the prepared cake pans, and smooth the tops.

Bake for 30 to 35 minutes (for the 8-in [20-cm] pans) or 25 to 30 minutes (for the 9-in [23-cm] pans), until a wooden skewer inserted into the center of each cake comes out clean or with just a few moist crumbs clinging to it.

Transfer the pans to wire racks and let cool for 10 minutes. Invert the cakes onto the racks, discard the parchment paper, and let cool completely, about 2 hours. (If you are making the layers a day in advance, when cool, wrap well in plastic wrap and store at room temperature overnight.)

TO FINISH THE CAKE: One hour before serving, in a food processor fitted with the metal chopping blade, combine the cold cream and the 1½ cups [600 ml] dulce de leche with the vanilla bean paste, vanilla extract, and rum (cream whipped in the food processor is denser and less fluffy than cream whipped with an electric mixer). Give the cream and dulce de leche 1 or 2 short pulses, just to combine. Continue to give the cream 1 or 2 pulses at a

Continued

time until it is no longer liquid and the consistency thickens, with a soft, dense, spreadable texture. Don't overbeat, or the cream will become grainy.

In a microwave-safe bowl, microwave 2¼ cups [520 g] dulce de leche for about 10 to 15 seconds on high heat, just until it is warm enough to spread easily.

Place one cake layer on a cake plate or pedestal, bottom-side up, and spread evenly with one-third of the warm dulce de leche, allowing any excess to drip down the sides of the cake. Top with about one-third of the sliced bananas, enough to cover the surface of the cake. Spread one-third of the whipped cream over the bananas. Place the second cake layer over the cream bottom-side up, and spread with another one-third of the warm dulce de leche, more sliced bananas, and another one-third of the whipped cream. Top with the final cake layer. Drizzle the final cake layer with just half of the remaining dulce de leche and spoon the last of the whipped cream on top of the cake in big dollops. Top the cream with a few banana slices and drizzle with the remaining dulce de leche. Serve immediately, or refrigerate for up to 1 hour to keep the whipped cream fresh.

Pudding as frosting? It sounds almost too decadent. I was inspired by the classic Brooklyn blackout cake when I created this three-layer beauty. The filling and frosting is a dense custard, with Dutch-process cocoa and lots of melted dark chocolate adding intensity and plenty of structure. For the best texture, make the chocolate pudding one day before you need it to fill and frost your cake. Oil, (rather than butter) in the banana cake batter ensures the cake's texture will stay soft and tender even when served cold straight from the refrigerator, and it slices like a dream.

DARK CHOCOLATE-PUDDING BANANA CAKE

SERVES 8 TO 10

DARK CHOCOLATE PUDDING

6 egg yolks

2 cups [480 ml] heavy cream

1 tsp instant espresso powder

¼ cup [20 g] Dutch-process cocoa powder (see page 13)

1½ cups [300 g] sugar

3 Tbsp cornstarch

¼ tsp fine sea salt

1½ cups [360 ml] whole milk

8 oz [230 g] semisweet chocolate, finely chopped, or chocolate chips

1½ tsp vanilla extract

CAKE BATTER

3¼ cups [390 g] cake flour

2½ tsp baking powder

½ tsp baking soda

1¼ tsp fine sea salt

4 eggs, at room temperature

2¾ cups [550 g] sugar

1 cup [240 ml] canola or vegetable oil

1 Tbsp vanilla extract

2 cups [460 g] mashed overripe bananas

1 cup [240 ml] buttermilk

CHOCOLATE CURLS

8 oz [230 g] semisweet chocolate chips

Dutch-process cocoa powder (see page 13) for sprinkling

TO MAKE THE CHOCOLATE PUDDING:
In a large bowl, whisk together the egg yolks, cream, and espresso powder. Set aside.

In a large, heavy-bottomed saucepan, whisk together the cocoa powder, sugar, cornstarch, and salt. Gradually whisk in the milk until smooth. Place over medium heat and cook, stirring constantly, just until the mixture comes to a boil. Remove from the heat and slowly whisk the hot cocoa mixture into the egg yolks and cream. Transfer back to the saucepan and continue cooking over medium heat, stirring constantly, until the pudding comes to boil. Lower the heat to a simmer and continue stirring for 1 to 2 minutes, until the mixture is very thick. Do not simmer any longer than 2 minutes, as the

cornstarch will actually lose its thickening powers and the pudding will start to thin.

Remove the pan from the heat and pour the pudding through a large fine-mesh sieve into a large bowl. Stir in the chopped chocolate and vanilla until the chocolate is completely melted and the pudding is smooth. Cover the surface of the pudding with plastic wrap to prevent a skin from forming and refrigerate until very firm and cold, at least 2 hours and preferably overnight.

TO MAKE THE CAKE: Position a rack in the center of the oven. Preheat the oven to 350°F [180°C]. Coat three 8-in [20-cm] or 9-in [23-cm] round cake pans with non-stick cooking spray and line the bottoms with parchment paper.

Continued

In a medium bowl, sift together the cake flour, baking powder, baking soda, and salt. Set aside.

In a stand mixer fitted with the paddle attachment, beat the eggs and sugar together on medium speed until thick and fluffy, 3 to 4 minutes. With the mixer on medium-high speed, gradually add the oil, beating until combined. Beat in the vanilla and mashed bananas.

With the mixer on low speed, alternately add the dry ingredients in three additions and the buttermilk in two additions, beginning and ending with the dry ingredients and scraping down the sides of the bowl as necessary. Beat just until combined, 10 to 15 seconds after each addition. Divide the batter evenly between the prepared pans, using a spatula to smooth the tops.

Bake for 30 to 35 minutes, until a wooden skewer inserted into the center of each cake comes out clean.

Transfer the pans to wire racks and let cool for 10 minutes. Invert the cake layers onto the racks, discarding the parchment paper. Let cool completely. (If you are making the layers a day in advance, when cool, wrap them well in plastic wrap and store at room temperature overnight.)

TO MAKE THE CHOCOLATE CURLS: Place a rimmed baking sheet in the refrigerator for 15 minutes.

Spread the chocolate chips in a single layer on a microwave-safe dinner plate. Microwave on high power for 1 minute. Stir the chocolate until it is completely melted. If there are still a few chunks of chocolate unmelted, return to the microwave for 15-second increments as needed, stirring between each, until the chocolate is smooth.

Scrape the chocolate onto the backside of the cold baking sheet and use an offset spatula to spread in an even layer. When the chocolate is firm, but not hard, use a bench scraper to push small sections of chocolate down and away from you in one continuous motion to form a curl. If the chocolate spreads but doesn't curl, it is still too warm, so let it sit for another minute or two before trying again. (The chocolate curls can be stored in a covered container in the refrigerator for up to 1 week.)

TO FINISH THE CAKE: Place one of the cake layers, bottom-side up, on a cardboard cake circle, serving plate, or cake stand. Spread about one-fourth of the very cold pudding over the surface of the cake. Top with a second layer of cake, bottom-side up, and spread with one-fourth of the pudding. Top with the final cake layer and spread the top and sides of the cake with the remaining pudding. Arrange the chocolate curls in a pretty pile on top of the cake and sprinkle very lightly with cocoa powder. Cut into wedges and serve, or refrigerate the cake until ready to serve, up to 1 day.

My good friend Heather Nunnelly learned to make this cake from her grandmother Dixie Seith, in Waco, Texas. Dixie was an avid baker, in large part because her husband Elwood insisted on dessert with every meal—even breakfast. Heather uses a diminutive round cake pan to create a cake that resembles a stack of pancakes, with a brown sugar glaze cascading down the sides like syrup.

DIXIE'S STACK CAKE

SERVES 4 TO 6

1 cup [220 g] unsalted butter, at room temperature

2 cups [400 g] granulated sugar

2 eggs, at room temperature

1 tsp vanilla extract

3 cups [420 g] all-purpose flour, sifted

2 tsp baking soda

1 tsp baking powder

½ tsp fine sea salt

¾ cup [180 ml] buttermilk

1½ cups [345 g] mashed overripe bananas

2 Tbsp bourbon

BROWN SUGAR GLAZE

8 Tbsp [110 g] unsalted butter

1 cup [200 g] firmly packed dark brown sugar

4 Tbsp milk

½ cup [60 g] confectioners' sugar

2 Tbsp bourbon

Position a rack in the center of the oven. Preheat the oven to 350°F [180°C]. Coat three 6-in [15-cm] cake pans with nonstick cooking spray and line the bottoms with parchment paper.

In a stand mixer fitted with the paddle attachment, beat the butter and sugar on medium until light and creamy, 4 to 5 minutes. Scrape the sides of the bowl and beat in the eggs, one at a time, beating well after each addition. Beat in the vanilla.

In a large bowl, sift together the flour, baking soda, baking powder, and salt. With the mixer on low speed, beat the dry ingredients into the batter in three additions, alternating with the buttermilk in two additions, beating just until combined, 10 to 15 seconds after each addition. Fold the bananas and bourbon into the batter by hand, using a large rubber or silicone spatula. Divide half of the batter evenly between the three prepared pans (½ to ¾ cup [120 to 180 ml] per pan) and smooth the tops, reserving the remaining batter for a second set of cake layers.

Bake for 15 to 20 minutes, until golden brown and a wooden skewer inserted into the center of each cake comes out clean.

Transfer the pans to wire racks and let cool for 5 minutes. Unmold the cakes onto the racks to finish cooling, discarding the parchment paper. Wipe out the cake pans and coat again with nonstick cooking spray and line the bottoms with parchment paper. Divide the remaining batter evenly between the cake pans, spreading the tops smooth with a spatula, and bake, unmold, and cool as before.

TO MAKE THE GLAZE: In a medium saucepan over medium heat, melt the butter. Stir in the brown sugar and bring to a boil, stirring constantly, for 2 minutes. Add the milk, continuing to stir, and bring back to a boil. Remove from the heat and let cool until warm. Whisk in the confectioners' sugar and bourbon until smooth.

Place one cake layer on a rimmed cake plate, top-side up. Spread a little glaze over the first layer, allowing a little bit to drip over the sides. Continue stacking the cake layers, spreading glaze over each one and allowing it to spill down the sides of the cake. Serve immediately, or cover lightly with plastic wrap and store at room temperature for up to 2 days.

3 cups [420 g] all-purpose flour

2 tsp baking powder

1 tsp baking soda

1¼ tsp fine sea salt

1¼ cups [275 g] unsalted butter, at room temperature

1¾ cups [350 g] granulated sugar

1 cup [200 g] firmly packed dark brown sugar

4 eggs, at room temperature

2 tsp vanilla extract

¼ cup [60 ml] dark rum

2 cups [460 g] mashed overripe bananas

1 cup [240 g] sour cream or crème fraîche, at room temperature

CARAMEL SAUCE

2 cups [400 g] granulated sugar

⅛ tsp cream of tartar

¼ cup [60 ml] water

2 cups [480 ml] heavy cream

4 Tbsp [55 g] unsalted butter

2 tsp vanilla extract

½ tsp fine sea salt

3 Tbsp dark rum

BROWN SUGAR BUTTERCREAM

6 eggs

2 cups [400 g] firmly packed dark brown sugar

1 tsp vanilla extract

¼ tsp fine sea salt

3 cups [660 g] unsalted butter, at room temperature

2 Tbsp dark rum

BUTTERED PECANS

2 Tbsp unsalted butter

2 cups [240 g] pecan halves

½ cup [100 g] granulated sugar

¼ tsp Maldon sea salt

Mr. Darcy and Elizabeth Bennet, Rhett Butler and Scarlett O'Hara, Tarzan and Jane. Some couples just can't fight their destiny to be together. Banana and caramel are a love match made in heaven, this chapter of their romance kissed by sea salt and a whisper of rum. The many components for this cake may seem daunting at first, but each one is really fairly simple to make, and they can all be prepared over the course of a couple of days, making the process more manageable. The completed cake will stay moist and fresh for at least 2 days in the refrigerator. It's a beautiful cake, perfect for a grand affair.

SALTED CARAMEL– PECAN BANANA CAKE

SERVES 8 TO 10

Position a rack in the center of the oven. Preheat the oven to 350°F [180°C]. Coat two 9-in [23-cm] round cake pans with non-stick cooking spray and line the bottoms with parchment paper.

In a medium bowl, sift together the flour, baking powder, baking soda, and salt. Set aside.

In a stand mixer fitted with the paddle attachment, beat the butter with the granulated sugar and brown sugar on medium speed until light and creamy, 3 to 4 minutes. Add the eggs, one at a time, beating well after each addition. Scrape down the sides of the bowl and beat in the vanilla, rum, bananas, and sour cream. Decrease the speed to low and add the flour mixture, in three additions, beating after each, just until combined, 10 to 15 seconds. Do not overbeat, or the cake will be tough. Divide the batter evenly between the two prepared pans, using a spatula to spread the tops smooth.

Bake for 40 to 50 minutes, until the cakes are golden brown and a wooden skewer inserted into the center of each cake comes out clean.

Transfer the pans to wire racks to cool for 10 minutes. Invert the cakes onto the racks, discarding the parchment paper, and let cool completely. (If you are making the layers a day in advance, when cool, wrap well in plastic wrap and store at room temperature overnight.)

TO MAKE THE CARAMEL SAUCE: In a 3-qt [2.8-L] heavy-bottomed saucepan over medium heat, combine the granulated sugar, cream of tartar, and water. Cook, gently swirling the pan occasionally, until the sugar dissolves into a syrup and starts to change color. Do not stir the sugar while it is caramelizing, as this can cause crystallization. Increase the heat to high and boil until the syrup turns a deep amber color (350° to 355°F [177° to 179°C] on a candy thermometer), 4 to 5 minutes. (Watch carefully, as the caramel can burn easily.)

Immediately remove the pan from the heat and pour in the cream, stirring with a long-handled wooden spoon. Be careful to avoid splattering, as the caramel will bubble furiously at first when combined with the cream. Place the pan over medium-low heat and cook, stirring constantly, until the caramel thickens, 3 to 5 minutes. Remove the sauce from the heat and whisk in the butter, salt, and rum until smooth. Let cool completely. (The sauce can be covered and refrigerated for up to 1 week. Before using the caramel, make sure to warm it slightly until it is malleable but not hot, about 10 to 15 seconds in the microwave.)

TO MAKE THE BUTTERCREAM: Fill a large sauté pan or skillet with water and bring to a simmer over medium heat.

Combine the eggs and brown sugar in the bowl of a stand mixer and place the bowl in the pan of simmering water. Using a large balloon whisk, briskly whip the eggs and sugar together continuously (do not stop or the eggs might scramble) until the sugar is completely dissolved and the mixture is very thick and fluffy and hot to the touch, 3 to 5 minutes. (It should register between 120° and 140°F [50° and 60°C] on an instant-read candy thermometer.)

Remove the bowl from the simmering water and, using the whisk attachment on the stand mixer, beat the eggs at high speed until they triple in volume, form soft peaks, and the bottom of the bowl is completely cool to the touch, 10 to 13 minutes. Beat in the vanilla and salt, just until incorporated.

Decrease the mixer speed to medium and gradually beat in the softened butter, about 2 Tbsp at a time, beating well after each addition. Don't panic if the buttercream starts to liquefy or look curdled as you beat in the butter. It will magically emulsify into a smooth, silky frosting by the time the last bit of butter has been added. Trust me. When all the butter is in, slowly drizzle in the rum, beating constantly, just until combined.

When the buttercream is smooth and glossy, remove the bowl from the mixer and fold in one-third of the cooled caramel sauce (about 1 cup [240 ml]). Taste the buttercream as you add the caramel, adjusting the flavor to your taste. But don't add more than half of the caramel to the buttercream; you need to set aside enough to drizzle over the frosted cake. Set the buttercream aside.

TO MAKE THE BUTTERED PECANS: In a large sauté pan or skillet over medium heat, melt the butter. When the butter starts to bubble and turn brown, add the pecans and stir to coat. Sprinkle with the sugar and continue stirring until the sugar begins to melt. Add 1 tablespoon water and continue stirring until the sugar is completely melted and syrupy. Spread the nut mixture in an even layer on a rimmed baking sheet. Sprinkle with the Maldon sea salt and let cool completely.

TO FINISH THE CAKE: Using a long serrated knife, slice both cake layers in half horizontally (see page 21). Place one layer, cut-side up, on a cardboard cake round, serving plate, or cake stand.

Coarsely chop about half of the pecans. Transfer half of the buttercream to a small bowl and fold in the chopped pecans. Drizzle the first cake layer with 2 to 3 Tbsp caramel sauce, then spread one-third of the pecan buttercream evenly over the top. Place a second layer on top, cut-side down. Drizzle with another 2 to 3 Tbsp caramel sauce and spread with another one-third of the pecan buttercream. Top with a third layer of cake, cut-side up, drizzling with more caramel and spreading it with the remaining pecan buttercream. Top with the final cake layer, cut-side down. Using a small portion of the remaining caramel buttercream, cover the cake with a thin crumb coat (see page 21). Refrigerate the cake for 30 minutes to solidify the crumb coat. Frost the top and sides of the cake with the remaining caramel buttercream. Refrigerate the cake at this point until the buttercream is cold and very firm, about 2 hours.

If the remaining caramel sauce (you should have about 1 cup [240 ml]) is cold, warm it briefly until it is pourable but not boiling hot. Pour the remaining caramel sauce over the top of the chilled cake in a steady stream, allowing it to cover the surface of the cake and drip decoratively down the sides. Arrange the remaining buttered pecan halves decoratively on the top of the cake. Serve immediately or refrigerate the cake in a covered cake carrier for up to 2 days, allowing the cake to come to room temperature for 1 to 2 hours before slicing.

For years, my birthday cake of choice was a classic German chocolate cake. As much as I love chocolate, the true draw was always the sweet, gooey coconut frosting.

When it comes to coconut, few people are ambivalent. Like anchovies or professional wrestling, coconut inspires either passionate fans or diehard haters. Opinions are never lukewarm. As a proud member of Team Coconut, I adore its sweet, tropical flavor and slightly chewy texture, and look for every possible opportunity to stir it into cakes and frostings, cookies, pies, and custards. Bakers in the American South have known for generations that the perfect way to celebrate a special occasion is with a magnificent, multilayered coconut cake, frosted with sweet, frothy meringue or silky buttercream and a blizzard of grated coconut. Every time I take a bite, I say a silent thank-you to the first person who decided something tasty just might be inside that big, hairy, odd-looking, hard-to-crack nut.

COCONUT BASICS

There are so many wonderful ways to infuse your baking with the delectable, tropical flavor of coconut. Simultaneously familiar and exotic, coconut is currently enjoying an upswing in popularity. Grocery stores are packed with bags of coconut—both sweetened and unsweetened—that has been flaked, shredded, chipped, and dessicated. Newer coconut products like coconut oil and coconut butter are becoming more commonplace in everyday cooking and baking, and fresh coconuts are easy to find in the produce department of most well-stocked supermarkets.

Depending on the cake I am making, I use a variety of coconut preparations: sweetened, fancy shredded or flaked coconut (I love the long, elegant strands); unsweetened shredded coconut; fat, chunky unsweetened coconut chips or flakes; and frozen unsweetened shredded coconut (a good shortcut for freshly grated coconut, and a nice addition to coconut pastry cream). For added coconut flavor, I sometimes use a little coconut extract (alcohol-based, like vanilla extract). Try Boyajian coconut flavoring, Flavorganics organic coconut extract, or Frontier's coconut flavoring (oil-based) if you are adamantly opposed to using the more commonly available imitation coconut extracts on the market.

Fresh coconut that I grate myself is the gold standard, and my first choice when baking Grandma Robideaux's Coconut-Pecan Cake (page 56) and cakes frosted with Seven-Minute Frosting (page 15) or any other sweet, marshmallow-y meringue-style frostings. Look for coconuts with hard, fibrous brown shells that weigh between 1½ and 2 lb [680 and 910 g]. When you shake the coconut, you should hear a lot of liquid sloshing inside, and the coconut should feel heavy for its size.

TOASTED COCONUT

To toast sweetened flaked or shredded coconut or coconut flakes or chips, use a dry skillet set over medium heat. Add the coconut and stir constantly with a wooden spoon until golden brown, 3 to 4 minutes. Pour immediately onto a small plate to cool.

CANNED COCONUT MILK

For baking, use canned coconut milk, not refrigerated coconut-milk beverage. Cha-okoh and Aroy-D brands from Thailand are good choices. Never buy "lite" or "light" coconut milk, which is just full-fat coconut milk diluted with water.

COCONUT OIL

For baking I always choose unrefined, organic virgin coconut oil. It has a delicate coconut aroma and flavor. Solid at room temperature, it will liquefy when heated in the microwave: Place in a microwave-safe container and microwave on high until it is liquid enough to measure in fluid ounces or milliliters, 30 to 40 seconds. Store in the refrigerator after opening.

COCONUT BUTTER

Coconut butter is an unsweetened spreadable paste that packs a serious punch of concentrated coconut flavor. Like natural almond or peanut butters, it is made simply from ground coconut meat. You can find coconut butter in most natural-food markets next to other minimally processed nut butters.

CREAM OF COCONUT

This thick, sweetened coconut syrup is usually used to flavor tropical drinks like piña coladas. Coco Lopez is a popular brand, or you can make your own Homemade Cream of Coconut (right). Do not confuse sweetened cream of coconut with coconut cream, which is a thicker, richer version of unsweetened canned coconut milk.

HOMEMADE CREAM OF COCONUT

Cream of coconut is a thick, silky, intensely flavored and incredibly sweet coconut syrup found in a can. It is commonly used in tropical drinks like piña coladas, but is also used in baking. Most commercially prepared cream of coconut products contain additives to give the syrup viscosity and keep it from separating. My homemade version replicates the sweet intensity of the canned version, without all the additives. I combine coconut butter with coconut milk and a little virgin coconut oil and sugar to replicate the creamy texture of the popular canned variety.

¾ cup [180 ml] canned coconut milk
3 Tbsp organic virgin coconut oil
¼ cup [65 g] organic coconut butter
1½ cups [300 g] sugar

In a 2-qt [2-L] saucepan over medium-high heat, combine the coconut milk, coconut oil, coconut butter, and sugar. Cook, stirring constantly, until the coconut oil melts and the sugar dissolves, 2 to 3 minutes.

Increase the heat to high and bring the mixture to a boil. Stirring constantly, boil the coconut mixture for 1 minute. Decrease the heat to medium-low and simmer until the cream of coconut is very thick and syrupy but still pourable, about 5 minutes. Remove from the heat and let cool completely. Transfer to a covered jar and refrigerate for up to 1 week. If the mixture separates, stir until smooth before using.

If I close my eyes, I see palm trees swaying. This dreamy coconut loaf combines coconut oil and unsalted butter for a deeply flavorful, tender crumb. You could bake this coconut loaf with coconut oil alone, but the final cake is then slightly heavier and slightly more dense, so I prefer using equal parts coconut oil and butter instead. The coconut soak goes on sticky, but as it penetrates the cake, it dries to a velvety sheen. Definitely 'ono (that's "delicious," in Hawaiian)!

KONA COCONUT LOAF

SERVES 6 TO 8

1½ cups [210 g] all-purpose flour

1 tsp baking powder

½ tsp fine sea salt

½ cup [115 g] virgin coconut oil

½ cup [110 g] unsalted butter

4 eggs

1⅓ cups [265 g] sugar

1 tsp vanilla extract

½ tsp coconut extract (see page 46)

¼ cup [60 ml] coconut milk

1½ cups [90 g] sweetened shredded or flaked coconut

½ cup [70 g] chopped macadamia nuts (optional)

COCONUT SOAK

½ cup [120 ml] coconut milk

½ cup [100 g] sugar

¼ tsp coconut extract (see page 46)

Position a rack in the center of the oven. Preheat the oven to 350°F [180°C]. Coat a 9-by-5-in [23-by-12-cm] metal loaf pan with nonstick cooking spray. Line the pan with an 8½-by-15-in [21.5-by-38-cm] strip of parchment paper so it covers the bottom of the pan and hangs over the long sides.

In a medium bowl, sift together the flour, baking powder, and salt. Set aside.

In a small saucepan over medium-low heat, combine the coconut oil and butter and stir together just until they are melted. Remove from the heat and set aside.

In the bowl of a stand mixer fitted with the paddle attachment, combine the eggs and sugar and beat on low speed just until thick and smooth but not fluffy, about 1 minute. Beat in the vanilla and coconut extracts. With the mixer still on low speed, drizzle the coconut oil–butter mixture into the egg mixture, beating just until smooth.

Spoon about one-third of the dry ingredients into the batter, beating on low speed just until the flour is blended into the batter, 10 to 15 seconds. Add the remaining dry ingredients in two additions in the same way. By hand, using a rubber or silicone spatula, fold in the coconut milk, two-thirds of the shredded coconut, and the macadamia nuts just until combined. Be careful not to overmix, or the cake will be tough. Scrape the batter into the prepared pan and smooth the top with the spatula.

Bake for 10 minutes, then reduce the oven temperature to 325°F [165°C] and continue baking for 40 to 50 minutes, until a wooden skewer inserted into the center of the cake comes out clean or with just a few moist crumbs clinging to it.

Transfer the pan to a wire rack and let cool for 10 minutes. Then, grasping the overhanging parchment, lift the loaf out of the pan and set it on the cooling rack. Discard the parchment paper.

In a small skillet over medium heat, toast the remaining shredded coconut, stirring continuously with a wooden spoon, until crisp and golden brown, 3 to 4 minutes. Pour onto a small plate and let cool.

TO MAKE THE COCONUT SOAK: In a medium heavy-bottomed saucepan over medium heat, stir together the coconut milk, sugar, and coconut extract. Bring to a boil, stirring until the sugar dissolves and the mixture thickens to the consistency of pancake syrup, 4 to 5 minutes.

Poke the top of the cake all over with a wooden skewer. Brush the top and sides of the cake with the warm coconut soak, and sprinkle immediately with the toasted coconut. Let cool completely before slicing and serving, or wrap well in plastic wrap and store at room temperature for up to 3 days.

2 cups [280 g] all-purpose flour

1½ tsp baking powder

½ tsp fine sea salt

⅔ cup [160 g] sour cream

¼ cup [60 ml] cream of coconut, store-bought (see page 46) or homemade (page 47)

1 tsp vanilla extract

1 cup [220 g] unsalted butter, at room temperature

2 cups [400 g] sugar

4 eggs, at room temperature

COCONUT–CREAM CHEESE FROSTING

8 oz [230 g] cream cheese, at room temperature

6 Tbsp [85 g] unsalted butter, at room temperature

1 tsp vanilla extract

Pinch of fine sea salt

2 to 3 cups [240 to 360 g] confectioners' sugar

¼ cup [60 ml] cream of coconut, store-bought (see page 46) or homemade (page 47)

2 cups [120 g] large unsweetened coconut flakes, or sweetened shredded or flaked coconut

When I was a little girl, I was fascinated by Pepperidge Farm frozen layer cakes. I just could not understand how a cake could come straight from a grocery-store freezer to my dinner table frosted and decorated—as easy as an ice-cream bar, but a lot more festive. Pondering why their cakes were square instead of round occupied much too much space in my young mind, exacerbated no doubt by the fact that my mother rarely indulged my youthful Pepperidge Farm fantasies, and the cakes almost never made it into our grocery cart. My homage to "the Farm" is this simple, single-layer sour cream and coconut cake. Its firm, almost pound cake–like texture makes it easy to split, fill, and frost with coconut–cream cheese frosting. Sprinkle the frosted cake with large unsweetened coconut flakes, or go vintage and cover the whole thing in a shower of sweetened shredded or flaked coconut instead. Want to make a larger, more impressive four-layer cake? This recipe doubles easily.

VINTAGE COCONUT CAKE

SERVES 9 TO 12

Position a rack in the center of the oven. Preheat the oven to 325°F [165°C]. Coat a 9-in [23-cm] square baking pan with nonstick cooking spray and line the bottom with parchment paper.

In a medium bowl, sift together the flour, baking powder, and salt. Set aside.

In a small bowl, whisk together the sour cream, cream of coconut, and vanilla.

In a stand mixer fitted with the paddle attachment, cream together the butter and sugar on medium speed until light and fluffy, 3 to 4 minutes. Scrape down the sides of the bowl and add the eggs, one at a time, beating well after each addition.

With the mixer on low speed, beat in half of the dry ingredients, just until combined, 15 to 20 seconds. Beat all of the sour-cream mixture into the batter, just until combined. By hand, using a rubber or silicone spatula or large balloon whisk, fold in the remaining dry ingredients. Do not overmix or the cake will be tough. Scrape the batter into the prepared pan and spread evenly with an offset spatula.

Bake for 45 to 55 minutes, until a wooden skewer inserted into the center of the cake comes out clean or with just a few moist crumbs clinging to it.

Continued

Transfer the pan to a wire rack and let cool for 10 minutes. Invert the cake onto the wire rack, discard the parchment paper, and let cool completely.

TO MAKE THE FROSTING: In a stand mixer fitted with the paddle attachment, beat together the cream cheese and butter until fluffy, 2 to 3 minutes. Beat in the vanilla, salt, and 2 cups [240 g] of the confectioners' sugar. Beat in the cream of coconut. For frosting with a firmer texture, beat in the remaining 1 cup [120 g] confectioners' sugar.

TO FINISH THE CAKE: Using a long serrated knife, slice the cake in half horizontally (see page 21). Place one half of the cake, cut-side up, on a cake plate or cake stand. Spread the top evenly with one-third of the frosting. Top with the second layer, cut-side down. Frost the top and sides of the cake liberally with the remaining frosting. Sprinkle the top generously with the coconut flakes, and press more around the sides of the cake. (Note: If you don't want to split the cake, simply spread the frosting over the top, leaving the sides of the cake bare. Use the back of a spoon to give the frosting a few decorative swirls and sprinkle with the coconut.)

Serve immediately, or cover lightly with plastic wrap and refrigerate for up to 24 hours. Allow the cold cake to come to room temperature, 1 to 2 hours, before slicing.

The provenance of poke cakes goes back to the ancient days of the 1970s—the heyday of cake mixes, Jell-O, and Cool Whip. Colorful and easy to make, poke cakes are the white patent-leather go-go boots of the bakery case—kitschy and dated, but still fun. To transform a simple white sheet cake into a classic Jell-O Poke Cake, the handle of a wooden spoon, a chopstick, or a large two-pronged fork was used to poke deep holes all over the the top of the cake. One or two colorful Jell-O syrups were poured over the top, trickling into the cake like brightly colored streamers. Served ice cold and slathered in Cool Whip, poke cakes were a potluck and pool-party staple. Less colorful but still tasty, my modern-day version relies on a coconut milk–based pudding spiked with cream of coconut and coconut rum instead of Jell-O to trickle sweetly into all its nooks and crannies. Top the cake with real whipped cream, toasted coconut, and a jaunty maraschino cherry to heighten its nostalgic appeal.

TRIPLE-COCONUT POKE CAKE

SERVES 12

2¾ cups [385 g] all-purpose flour

2 cups [400 g] sugar

1 Tbsp baking powder

1 tsp fine sea salt

1 cup [220 g] unsalted butter, at room temperature, cut into 16 pieces

1⅓ cups [320 ml] canned coconut milk

6 egg whites, at room temperature

1 tsp vanilla extract

TRIPLE COCONUT PUDDING

2 cups [480 ml] canned coconut milk (or substitute 1 cup coconut milk plus 1 cup heavy cream for a richer pudding)

3 Tbsp cornstarch

3 egg yolks

½ cup [100 g] sugar

Pinch of salt

1½ cups [360 ml] cream of coconut, store-bought (see page 46) or homemade (page 47)

3 Tbsp coconut rum, such as Malibu

WHIPPED TOPPING

2 cups [480 ml] heavy cream

¼ cup [50 g] sugar, plus more if desired

1 tsp vanilla extract

1 to 1½ cups [60 to 90 g] toasted coconut (see page 46)

Maraschino cherries for serving (optional)

Position a rack in the center of the oven. Preheat the oven to 350°F [180°C]. Coat a 9-by-13-in [23-by-33-cm] baking pan with nonstick cooking spray.

In a stand mixer fitted with the paddle attachment, beat together the flour, sugar, baking powder, and salt on low speed. Add the butter and continue to beat on low until the mixture looks crumbled and sandy.

In a small bowl, stir together the coconut milk, egg whites, and vanilla with a fork. With the mixer still on low, add half of the coconut milk–egg white mixture, beating just until blended. Increase the mixer speed to medium-high and continue

beating for 2 minutes. Stop the mixer and scrape down the sides of the bowl.

Return the mixer speed to low, add half of the remaining coconut milk–egg white mixture, and beat for about 10 seconds, until fully blended. Finally, add the rest of the coconut milk–egg white mixture and beat the batter until thick and smooth, 10 to 15 seconds more. Scrape the batter into the prepared pan, spreading evenly.

Bake for 25 to 30 minutes, until a wooden skewer inserted into the center of the cake comes out clean. Transfer the pan to a wire rack and let cool.

Continued

TO MAKE THE PUDDING: In a medium bowl, combine ¼ cup [60 ml] of the coconut milk and the cornstarch and stir to dissolve. Whisk in the egg yolks until smooth. Set aside.

In a 3-qt [2.8-L] saucepan over medium heat, combine the remaining 1¾ cups [420 ml] coconut milk, the sugar, and the salt. Cook, stirring, until the coconut milk comes to a boil.

Remove the pan from the heat and whisk the hot coconut milk mixture into the egg yolk mixture, ¼ cup [60 ml] at a time, until thoroughly combined (adding the hot milk to the eggs gradually will prevent the eggs from curdling). When the milk is completely whisked into the yolks, return the entire mixture to the saucepan and cook, whisking constantly, until the pudding comes to a gentle boil and starts to thicken. Continue whisking and cook for 1 to 2 minutes. Remove from the heat and stir in the cream of coconut and the coconut rum.

Poke deep holes all over the cake, using the pointed end of a chopstick or the handle of a wooden spoon. Pour the warm pudding evenly over the surface of the cake, spreading it smoothly with a small offset spatula. Let the cake cool to room temperature, allowing the pudding to soak into the cake. Cover with plastic wrap and refrigerate until very cold, at least 2 hours but preferably overnight.

TO MAKE THE TOPPING: Chill a large bowl and the beaters of an electric mixer for 15 minutes. Combine the cream, sugar, and vanilla in the chilled bowl and beat until stiff peaks form (add more sugar to taste if you prefer a sweeter topping).

TO FINISH THE CAKE: Spread the whipped topping evenly over the chilled cake and sprinkle with the toasted coconut. Cut into squares and serve. Go completely retro and top each serving with a maraschino cherry, if you like. To store, cover the pan loosely with plastic wrap and refrigerate for up to 3 days.

My grandmother's special recipe for coconut cake calls for a combination of vegetable shortening and butter in the cake batter. She used butter for flavor and shortening for a lighter, fluffier texture. The frosted cake becomes more tender and tastes best when it's given a day or two to age and ripen before you serve it. Store the frosted cake at room temperature, in a tightly covered cake carrier.

GRANDMA ROBIDEAUX'S COCONUT-PECAN CAKE

SERVES 8 TO 10

½ cup [110 g] unsalted butter, at room temperature

6 Tbsp [85 g] vegetable shortening, at room temperature

3 cups [600 g] sugar

2 eggs, separated, plus 2 egg yolks

1½ tsp vanilla extract

2¾ cups [385 g] all-purpose flour

2 tsp baking powder

1 tsp fine sea salt

1¾ cups [420 ml] whole milk

2 cups [240 g] pecan halves, toasted (see page 16) and finely chopped

MARSHMALLOW-MERINGUE FROSTING

1½ cups [300 g] sugar

1 tsp light corn syrup

⅔ cup [160 ml] boiling water

2 egg whites

9 large marshmallows

1 tsp vanilla extract

3 to 4 cups [180 to 240 g] freshly grated coconut (see page 46)

Position a rack in the center of the oven. Preheat the oven to 350°F [180°C]. Coat three 8-in [20-cm] round cake pans with nonstick cooking spray and line the bottoms with parchment paper.

In a stand mixer fitted with the paddle attachment, beat together the butter, shortening, and sugar until pale and creamy, 4 to 5 minutes. Beat in the egg yolks (a total of 4), one at a time, beating well after each addition. Scrape down the sides of the bowl. Beat in the vanilla.

In a medium bowl, sift together the flour, baking powder, and salt.

Add one-third of the dry ingredients to the batter, beating on low speed just until the flour blends into the batter, 15 to 20 seconds. Beat in half of the milk. Add the remaining dry ingredients and then the remaining milk, beating each addition just until incorporated. Be careful not to

overbeat the batter or the cake will be tough. Fold in the chopped nuts by hand using a rubber or silicone spatula.

In a medium bowl, using a handheld electric mixer, beat the 2 egg whites to soft peaks. Fold the egg whites into the batter, just until combined. Divide the batter evenly between the prepared pans and smooth the tops with the spatula.

Bake for 22 to 25 minutes, until a wooden skewer inserted into the center of each cake comes out clean.

Transfer the pans to wire racks and let cool for 10 minutes. Invert the cakes onto the racks, discard the parchment paper, and let cool completely.

TO MAKE THE FROSTING: In a medium saucepan over medium-high heat, combine the sugar, corn syrup, and boiling water. Cook, without stirring but swirling the pan occasionally, until the sugar dissolves and the syrup comes to a boil. Cook until the syrup reaches 240°F [115°C] on a candy thermometer, about 5 minutes.

Meanwhile, when the syrup reaches about 200°F [95°C], in a stand mixer fitted with the whisk attachment, start beating the egg whites at medium speed. When the egg whites reach soft peaks and the syrup reaches 240°F [115°C], increase the mixer speed to high and add the syrup to the egg whites in a steady stream, beating until the meringue is thick and glossy and forms stiff, curling peaks when the beaters are lifted but is still warm. Still beating, add the marshmallows, one at a time, beating well after each addition, until they have melted into the frosting mixture. After all the marshmallows are added, beat in the vanilla. Use the frosting immediately.

TO FINISH THE CAKE: Place the first cake layer on a cake plate or pedestal bottom-side up. Working quickly, generously frost the first layer with about one-fourth of the frosting and sprinkle with ⅓ to ½ cup [20 to 30 g] of the coconut. Top with the second cake layer, bottom-side down, spreading it with about one-fourth of the frosting and sprinkling with more coconut. Top with the third layer, bottom-side up, and frost the top and sides of the cake with the remaining frosting. Press the remaining coconut thickly on the top and sides of the cake, or as desired.

Store the cake at room temperature in a covered cake carrier and allow it to age for 24 to 36 hours before serving.

A SWEET FAMILY HEIRLOOM

My great-grandma Robideaux lived to be 111 years old, and she ate dessert every day of her life. She was a wonderful baker and an avid, if unromantic, gardener. With the exception of the Shasta daisies that grew clustered around her front porch, she refused to grow anything you couldn't eat. She lived the farm-to-table life before it was fashionable. A native Louisianan, she resettled in Santa Cruz, California, with my great-grandfather in 1930, raising all her own vegetables in a lush and meticulously organized backyard garden.

As impressive as her garden was, when we were invited for Sunday dinner, my brothers and I could only endure the long afternoon filled with dull adult conversation and nothing to watch on television other than golf or Mutual of Omaha's *Wild Kingdom*, with the promise that my great-grandmother would bake. We couldn't wait to see what she would serve for dessert. Well into her eighties, my grandmother baked for everyone who came calling. What she served was always a surprise; there were pies packed with wild blackberries she foraged for along the road in her neighborhood, delicate fig bars made from jam she canned herself, and little chocolate pound cakes encased in a thin, crackling sugar glaze.

We all had our favorite, but the dessert I craved and always requested if I was lucky enough to be asked, was her coconut-pecan cake. It seems there are as many coconut-cake recipes in the South as there are stars in the sky, and my grandmother's recipe is well over one hundred years old, handed down to her from her own mother. The cake was a true labor of love, a three-layered beauty made with fresh coconut grated by hand on the tiniest holes of a box grater, the sweet batter packed with an extravagance of finely chopped toasted pecans. Whenever she received a bag of the hard-shelled nuts from her sister back home in Louisiana and tasked my great-grandfather with cracking them, painstakingly picking the precious meat from the broken shells, I knew it wouldn't be long before three layers of coconut perfection were on my plate.

Unlike most coconut cakes which are best eaten the same day they are iced with a sugary meringue frosting, my grandmother liked to let her cake sit a day or two before she allowed anyone to cut the first slice. The flavors deepened, the texture grew more tender, and the thick halo of fluffy marshmallow meringue slathered over its layers gradually absorbed the flavor of the fresh coconut and lost its glossy pompadour sheen, slumping a little before settling gracefully into a velvety sheath around the cake. It was a quietly elegant cake, sitting regally on the old dining room sideboard, secure in its indisputable desirability. Although the crown jewel of her Sunday dinner, there were other desserts of lesser status set around the cake stand—like drones buzzing around the queen bee—to ensure no one's sweet tooth went unsatisfied, but mostly to ensure devoted coconut-pecan cake acolytes like me were assured a second piece.

2 cups [280 g] all-purpose flour

2 tsp baking powder

¼ tsp baking soda

¾ tsp fine sea salt

4 oz [115 g] unsweetened chocolate, coarsely chopped

¼ cup [20 g] natural cocoa powder (see page 13)

¾ cup [180 ml] organic virgin coconut oil

1 cup [240 ml] water

3 eggs

2¼ cups [250 g] granulated sugar

2 tsp vanilla extract

½ cup [120 g] sour cream

COCONUT-FLUFF FILLING

1 cup [220 g] unsalted butter, at room temperature

2 cups [240 g] confectioners' sugar, sifted

1 Tbsp cream of coconut, store-bought (see page 46) or homemade (page 47)

½ tsp vanilla extract

Pinch of fine sea salt

One 7-oz [200-g] jar marshmallow cream, such as Marshmallow Fluff

3 cups [180 g] sweetened shredded or flaked coconut

2 or 3 drops pink food coloring

COCONUT-MARSHMALLOW TOPPING

1 cup [240 ml] cold water

3 Tbsp unflavored granulated gelatin

1⅓ cups [265 g] granulated sugar

¾ cup [240 g] light corn syrup

Fine sea salt

1 tsp vanilla extract

⅛ tsp coconut extract (see page 46)

Hostess SnoBall fans, rejoice! Here is a giant, grown-up version of your favorite lunch-box snack, imbued with coconut throughout—from the fudgy cake and creamy filling to the tender, spongy marshmallow swathing its generous curves. This cake must be made at least a day ahead of serving, to give the marshmallow enough time to set.

COCONUT-FUDGE SNOWBALL

SERVES 8 TO 10

Position a rack in the center of the oven. Preheat the oven to 350°F [180°C]. Coat one 2-qt [2-L] ovenproof bowl (stainless-steel or Pyrex) and one 9-in [23-cm] round cake pan with nonstick cooking spray. Line the bottom of the cake pan with parchment paper.

In a medium bowl, sift together the flour, baking powder, baking soda, and salt. Set aside.

In a medium saucepan over medium-low heat, combine the unsweetened chocolate, cocoa powder, coconut oil, and water, stirring occasionally, just until the chocolate and coconut oil are melted and the mixture is smooth. Set aside to cool slightly.

In a stand mixer fitted with the whisk attachment, beat the eggs on low speed until frothy. With the mixer running, gradually add the sugar. Increase the mixer speed to high and continue beating until the eggs are pale, fluffy, and tripled in volume, about 4 minutes. Beat in the vanilla. With the mixer off, scrape the

melted chocolate mixture into the batter. With the mixer on low speed, beat just until smooth.

Turn off the mixer and add half of the dry ingredients. Beat on low speed for 15 to 20 seconds, just until incorporated. Turn off the mixer and scrape down the sides of the bowl. With the mixer on low speed, beat in the sour cream. Add the remaining dry ingredients and beat just until the batter is smooth, 10 to 15 seconds. Divide the batter evenly between the prepared bowl and the cake pan, and smooth the tops.

Bake for 28 to 35 minutes, until a wooden skewer inserted into the center of each cake comes out clean. (The cake baked in the bowl may take a little longer to bake than the layer baked in the cake pan.)

Transfer the pans to wire racks and let cool completely.

Continued

TO MAKE THE COCONUT-FLUFF FILLING:
In a stand mixer fitted with the paddle attachment, beat together the butter and confectioners' sugar on medium-low speed until slightly crumbly. Add the cream of coconut, vanilla, and salt. Increase the mixer speed to high and beat for 2 to 3 minutes, until light and creamy.

With a rubber or silicone spatula, scrape the marshmallow fluff from the jar and gently fold into the buttery mixture by hand, taking care not to deflate the fluffy texture of the marshmallow. Set aside.

With a sharp paring knife, cut a circle about 5 in [12 cm] in diameter in the center of the bowl cake, starting about 2 in [5 cm] from the edge. Use a spoon to carve out the circle into a hole 2 to 3 in [5 to 7.5 cm] deep. Fill the hole with the coconut fluff, skimming a thin layer of fluff over the cake border as well, to help the second layer adhere. Top the bowl cake with the 9-in [23-cm] cake layer, covering the filling, and invert the entire cake onto a cardboard cake round, cake platter, or cake stand.

In a self-sealing plastic bag, combine the shredded coconut with the food coloring, shaking it and massaging the color in evenly. Set aside.

TO MAKE THE COCONUT-MARSHMALLOW TOPPING: Pour ½ cup [120 ml] of the cold water into the bowl of a stand mixer fitted with the whisk attachment. Sprinkle the gelatin evenly over the water and allow it to sit and absorb the water, 15 to 20 minutes.

In a medium saucepan over low heat, combine the remaining ½ cup [120 ml] water, the granulated sugar, the corn syrup, and the salt. Cook, swirling the pan occasionally, until the sugar dissolves. Increase the heat to high and let the syrup come to a boil. Cook, without stirring, until it reaches 238° to 240°F [114° to 115°C] on a candy thermometer. Remove the syrup from the heat. With the mixer on low, slowly beat the syrup into the gelatin.

After the syrup is added, increase the mixer speed to high and continue beating until the marshmallow is thick, fluffy, and very white but still warm, 10 to 13 minutes. Beat in the vanilla and coconut extracts.

While the coconut-marshmallow topping is still warm, using a rubber or silicone spatula, scrape all of the topping on top of the cake. Using an offset spatula, very quickly spread it over the cake in a smooth, even layer. While the marshmallow is still warm and sticky, immediately sprinkle it with the tinted coconut, pressing it into the marshmallow as needed to help it stick. Let the cake sit, undisturbed, allowing the marshmallow to cure uncovered at room temperature, for 8 to 12 hours before serving.

Store in a covered cake carrier at room temperature for up to 2 days.

My oldest daughter, Olivia, is an actress and a romantic by nature, so for her twenty-first birthday, I made her a luxuriously rich coconut cake filled with mascarpone and tart passion fruit—to celebrate both her special day and her vibrant personality. The coconut buttercream is scented delicately with a tiny splash of rose water, and I decorated the cake with an extravagant number of fresh pink rosebuds to echo that flavor. It's a flamboyant but surprisingly easy way to decorate a cake, and requires no special cake-decorating skills. Try to find organic and pesticide-free roses if you are going to do this, but you can play it safe and wrap the cut stems with floral tape as added protection before plunging the flowers into the cake. Take care when adding the rose water to the buttercream—it's very potent and aromatic; a drop or two goes a very long way.

COCONUT PASSION

SERVES 8 TO 10

Position a rack in the center of the oven. Preheat the oven to 350°F [180°C]. Coat three 9-in [23-cm] round cake pans with nonstick cooking spray and line the bottoms with parchment-paper.

In a medium bowl, sift together the flour, baking powder, and salt. Set aside.

In a food processor fitted with the metal blade, combine the sugar and coconut and process until the coconut is very, very finely ground. Set aside.

In a small bowl, whisk together the vanilla and coconut extracts, sour cream, and coconut milk. Set aside.

In a stand mixer fitted with the paddle attachment, cream the butter on low speed for about 30 seconds. Add the coconut-infused sugar and continue beating until

light and fluffy, 3 to 5 minutes. Scrape down the sides of the bowl.

With the mixer on medium speed, beat in the eggs, one at a time, beating well after each addition. Add the dry ingredients in three additions, alternating with the sour cream mixture in two additions, beginning and ending with the dry ingredients and beating for 10 to 15 seconds after each addition, just until combined. Divide the batter evenly between the prepared pans and smooth the tops with an offset spatula.

Bake for 25 to 30 minutes, until a wooden skewer inserted into the center of each cake comes out clean.

TO MAKE THE PASSION FRUIT SYRUP:
While the cake is baking, in a 2-qt [2-L] saucepan over medium heat, stir together the sugar and water. Bring to a boil and

3 cups [420 g] all-purpose flour

3 tsp baking powder

1 tsp fine sea salt

2¾ cups [550 g] sugar

1 cup [60 g] sweetened shredded or flaked coconut

2 tsp vanilla extract

½ tsp coconut extract (see page 46)

½ cup [120 g] sour cream or crème fraîche, at room temperature

¾ cup [180 ml] coconut milk or whole milk, at room temperature

1½ cups [330 g] unsalted butter, at room temperature

6 eggs, at room temperature

PASSION FRUIT SYRUP

¾ cup [150 g] sugar

1 cup [240 ml] water

⅓ cup [80 ml] passion fruit purée

PASSION FRUIT CURD

8 egg yolks

1 cup [200 g] sugar

2 Tbsp fresh lemon juice

⅛ tsp fine sea salt

½ cup [120 ml] passion fruit purée

½ cup [110 g] unsalted butter, at room temperature

COCONUT-MASCARPONE FILLING

1 cup [240 g] mascarpone cheese

¼ cup [60 ml] cream of coconut, store-bought (see page 46) or homemade (page 47)

⅔ cup [160 ml] heavy cream

COCONUT-ROSE BUTTERCREAM

6 eggs

2 cups [400 g] sugar

⅛ tsp fine sea salt

3 cups [660 g] unsalted butter, at room temperature

¼ cup [60 ml] cream of coconut, store-bought (see page 46) or homemade (page 47), plus more if desired

⅛ tsp rose water or 2 tsp vanilla extract

Fresh roses (preferably organic and pesticide-free) to cover the top of the cake

Continued

cook for 1 minute. Add the passion fruit purée and simmer until syrupy, about 2 minutes. Set aside.

When the cakes are done, transfer the pans to wire racks and let cool for 10 minutes. Invert the cakes onto the racks, discarding the parchment paper. While the cake layers are still warm, brush the top and sides of each one liberally with the warm passion fruit syrup, making sure to use all of the syrup. Set aside and let cool completely.

TO MAKE THE PASSION FRUIT CURD:
In a 2-qt [2-L] stainless-steel bowl, whisk together the egg yolks, sugar, lemon juice, salt, and passion fruit purée. Place the bowl over a 3-qt [2.8-L] saucepan of simmering water. Cook the curd, whisking continuously, until the mixture is thick and coats the back of a spoon. Whisk in the butter, 2 Tbsp at a time, until smooth.

Pour the curd through a fine-mesh sieve into a clean bowl. Cover the curd with plastic wrap, pressing it onto the surface to prevent a skin from forming, and refrigerate until very cold, at least 2 hours or up to overnight.

TO MAKE THE COCONUT-MASCARPONE FILLING:
In a medium bowl, stir together the mascarpone and cream of coconut until smooth. In a separate medium bowl, using an electric hand mixer set at medium speed, beat the heavy cream to soft peaks. Fold the mascarpone mixture and whipped cream together with a rubber or silicone spatula just until smooth. Do not overmix or the mascarpone will become grainy. Set aside.

TO MAKE THE COCONUT-ROSE BUTTER-CREAM:
Fill a large sauté pan or skillet with water and bring to a simmer over medium heat. In the bowl of a stand mixer, combine the eggs, sugar, and salt. Place the mixer bowl in the pan of simmering water. Using a large balloon whisk, briskly whip the egg mixture (do not stop whisking or the eggs will scramble) until the sugar is completely dissolved and the mixture is thick and fluffy and very hot to the touch, 3 to 5 minutes. Use an instant-read candy thermometer to check the temperature; it should register between 120° and 140°F [50° to 60°C].

Remove the bowl from the simmering water and, using the stand mixer fitted with the whisk attachment, beat the egg mixture at high speed until they triple in volume, soft, fluffy peaks form, and the bottom of the bowl is completely cool to the touch, 10 to 13 minutes.

Decrease the mixer speed to medium and gradually beat in the softened butter, 2 Tbsp at a time, beating well after each addition. Don't panic if the buttercream starts to liquefy or look curdled as you beat in the butter. It will magically emulsify into a smooth, silky frosting by the time the last bit of butter has been added. I promise. When all the butter has been added to the buttercream, slowly drizzle in the cream of coconut, beating until smooth. Add the rose water a few drops at a time (literally, by the drop—once you have added too much rose water there is no turning back) until the desired flavor is reached. If you want a stronger coconut flavor, fold in a little more cream of coconut, 1 Tbsp at a time.

TO FINISH THE CAKE:
Fit a large disposable piping bag with a large round tip. Fill the bag with one-fourth of the buttercream.

Place one cake layer on a cardboard cake round, cake platter, or cake stand. Pipe a thick border of the buttercream around the edge of the cake to form a dam. Spread ½ cup [120 g] to ¾ cup [180 g] of the mascarpone filling in an even layer inside the dam and top with ½ cup [120 g] to ¾ cup [180 g] of the passion fruit curd, spreading it evenly. The buttercream dam will prevent the soft fillings from leaking. Top with the next cake layer. Pipe a buttercream dam around the edge of the second layer in the same manner and fill with the remaining mascarpone filling and then the passion fruit curd. Top with the final cake layer. Refrigerate the cake for 15 to 30 minutes to let the fillings set.

Spread the top and sides of the cake with a thin layer of the buttercream to form a crumb coat (see page 21). Refrigerate for 30 minutes, or until the buttercream is firm.

Spread the remaining buttercream generously over the top and sides of the cake, smoothing it evenly. (The cake can be assembled and refrigerated for up to 24 hours before finishing the decorating.)

About 2 hours before serving, cut the rose stems to a length of 1½ in [4 cm] each, removing any leaves and thorns. Wrap the stems tightly with floral tape and plunge them decoratively into the cake, covering the top completely with flowers. Let come to room temperature before cutting into slices and serving.

Remove the flowers and refrigerate for up to 2 days.

CHOCOLATE

A newspaper headline recently caught my eye: "Chocolate cake for breakfast could help you lose weight." Was I seeing things? Is that the "Hallelujah Chorus" I hear singing? And really, could there be a cheerier, more life-affirming sight first thing in the morning than a thickly frosted chocolate layer cake sitting on your kitchen counter? There is no fan club more ardent than the one devoted to chocolate. For many people, when it comes to cake, chocolate is the only flavor they ever crave. And like the grande dame that she is, chocolate is happy to be all things to all people. Irresistible on its own, chocolate plays well with other flavors, too—from toasty malt, rich coffee, and peanut butter to caramel, vanilla bean, and fresh fruit like raspberries, strawberries, and ripe bananas. You might think the perfect start to your day is a steaming cup of hot coffee or a perfectly poached egg, but I beg to differ. I vote for chocolate cake.

CHOCOLATE BASICS

Picking out your favorite chocolate used to be as simple as choosing dark, milk, or white. But the growing diversity of artisanal chocolates, and the terminology used for describing them, is ever growing. To untangle the confusion, here is a quick explanation for some of the language used to describe chocolate.

CHOCOLATE PERCENTAGES

When you see a percentage plastered on the label of your chocolate bar, it isn't necessarily a measure of the bar's quality. It simply identifies the percentage of cacao in the chocolate in relation to other ingredients, mainly sugar. Cacao, or the chocolate liqueur made when roasted cacao nibs are ground into a thick liquid, is equal parts cocoa powder and cocoa butter. Cocoa powder provides the chocolaty flavor we're familiar with and cocoa butter, an almost flavorless fat, provides the creamy texture. Chocolatiers may play with the ratio of cocoa butter and cocoa powder in their chocolate, but whatever the combination of the two, this adds up to the cacao percentage in the bar. Unsweetened chocolate is 100 percent cacao, and is usually a 50/50 split between cocoa powder and cocoa butter. On the other end of the spectrum, milk chocolate is made with milk solids and vanilla, along with a greater percentage of sugar and a lower percentage of cacao.

It's true that a chocolate with a higher percentage of cacao, like an 80 percent or 72 percent chocolate bar, will be more intense and bittersweet than a semisweet bar labeled 56 percent to 62 percent cacao, simply because it contains less sugar. But other factors go into the chocolate bar's flavor and complexity, including the origin of the cocoa beans, how the cacao nibs are roasted, and the ratio of cocoa powder versus cocoa butter in the bar. In other words, all chocolate bars labeled 70 percent cacao aren't necessarily created equal.

COUVERTURE

Translating to "covering" chocolate, couverture is fine, professional-grade chocolate that uses high-quality cocoa beans. It is usually produced with a higher proportion of cocoa butter to ensure smooth melting and a glossy finish.

SINGLE ORIGIN CHOCOLATE

Many chocolates are made from a blend of cocoa beans from different countries, so a "single origin" label indicates that the chocolate is made with cocoa beans from one particular country or region. The flavor of the chocolate, like wine or coffee, reflects the terroir, or character of the soil, the climate, and the environment where the beans are grown.

WHITE CHOCOLATE

A controversial confection that chocolate connoisseurs either love or loathe, white chocolate isn't technically chocolate, since it is made with only cocoa butter, without any of the cocoa solids that give dark chocolate its flavor. But with its creamy sweetness and chocolaty texture, I still think it deserves a place in every chocolate lover's heart.

GO-TO GANACHE

It's a glaze! It's a filling! It's a buttercream! Chocolate reaches true superstar status in the classic French preparation for chocolate ganache. I adore chocolate ganache for its ease and versatility. At its most elemental, it is just a simple combination of finely chopped chocolate melted together with warm cream and whisked into a smooth sauce. You can enrich it with a knob of butter, make it glossy with a spoonful of corn syrup or honey, or add pizzazz with a splash of whiskey, bourbon, or dark rum. Given time to set, ganache makes both an excellent filling and frosting for layer cakes.

8 oz [230 g] semisweet chocolate (60 to 62 percent cacao), finely chopped

1 cup [240 ml] heavy cream

1 tsp vanilla extract

Possible additions (do not use if making caramel ganache, below): 1 Tbsp butter and 1 Tbsp corn syrup or honey (for shine); 1 to 2 Tbsp whiskey, bourbon, dark rum, or brandy (for added flavor)

Place the chocolate in a medium heatproof bowl. In a small saucepan over medium-high heat, bring the cream to a boil. Immediately pour the cream over the chocolate. Let sit for 1 minute, then add the vanilla and gently whisk until smooth. Whisk in the butter, corn syrup, and/or whiskey, if using, until smooth.

Ganache can be made ahead of time and stored in the refrigerator in a tightly covered container for up to 1 week. Allow it to come to room temperature until soft enough to spread, or melt back into a sauce by microwaving on high for about 1 minute.

VERSATILE GANACHE

You can do so many things with ganache. Here are a few of my favorites:

- Pour barely warm ganache over an unfrosted single layer cake as a glaze.

- Pour warm ganache over ice cream or slices of cake as a sauce.

- Let cool slightly and pour over the top of a double- or triple-layer frosted cake: spread it over the top with a flat or off-set metal spatula, and let excess glaze drip prettily halfway down the sides of the cake.

- Let cool completely at room temperature (8 to 12 hours) until thick and spreadable. Then use to fill or frost a double-layer cake—or both!

- Fold whipped cream into ganache that has cooled but not set, for a quickie chocolate mousse.

- For caramel ganache, try substituting 1½ cups [360 ml] warm bourbon-infused homemade caramel sauce (see page 85) for the heavy cream in the recipe at left.

- Turn ganache into chocolate buttercream: With an electric mixer, beat 1 cup [220 g] softened unsalted butter into the cooled and set ganache, 2 Tbsp at a time, until fluffy and creamy. Caramel ganache makes a particularly luscious buttercream.

COCOA POWDER 101

When cocoa butter is extracted from cocoa liqueur, the remaining cocoa solids are dried and finely ground into cocoa powder. Some of the deepest, darkest, most intensely flavored chocolate cakes are made exclusively with cocoa powder. Cocoa powder has a deep, intense chocolate flavor that isn't masked by the addition of cocoa butter or sugar.

Natural cocoa: Natural unsweetened cocoa powder is the most popular type of cocoa in the United States, with Hershey's being the most prominent brand. It is intensely flavored, slightly fruity, and very acidic. In cake recipes, cocoa powder is often dissolved in a hot liquid to help the flavor "bloom." Natural cocoa has an affinity for other acidic ingredients like sour cream, buttermilk, and coffee, and cakes made with natural cocoa are always leavened with baking soda or a combination of baking soda and baking powder. When moistened and then combined with an acidic ingredient like natural cocoa, baking soda immediately begins to form carbon dioxide gas that enlarges the air pockets already beaten into the batter, helping the cake to rise.

Dutch-process cocoa: In the nineteenth century, Dutchman Coenraad Johannes van Houten invented a process to wash cocoa beans in an alkaline (low-acid) solution to temper their bitterness and acidity before the beans were shelled and ground. Alkalized cocoa has a smoother, richer flavor and a much darker color than natural cocoa. Since Dutch-process cocoa (sometimes referred to simply as European-style cocoa) is no longer acidic, baking powder is usually the only leavening

agent needed. In fact, the combination of alkalized cocoa and baking soda can give your cake a salty, soapy taste if there aren't enough other acidic ingredients in the batter to activate the baking soda.

Black cocoa: This specialty cocoa is "ultra-Dutch-processed" and is very dark, almost black in color. The flavor is very mellow and the color so dark, it should only be used as an accent in combination with traditional Dutch-process cocoa or natural cocoa powder.

Blended cocoa: With the growing popularity of European-style cocoa, many companies are developing cocoa blends that combine the best of both worlds—Dutch-process and natural cocoas combined into one blended cocoa powder. Hershey's developed their Special Dark formula, and companies like King Arthur Flour have five or six different cocoa blends to satisfy every baking need. These blended cocoa powders retain the acidity of natural cocoa combined with the deep, dark color and mellow richness of Dutch-process. Blended cocoa is versatile enough to use in most recipes, no matter what type of cocoa or leavening agents the recipe might originally call for.

You are spoiled for choice when hunting for a bold stout beer to use in this handsome chocolate loaf. There are chocolate stouts and coffee stouts and big breakfast stouts brewed with oatmeal *and* coffee. You could use a syrupy black Imperial stout or a dry Irish stout like Guinness. But my stout-of-choice for this deep, dark chocolate cake is a velvety milk stout. Milk stouts are brewed with unfermentable sugars, like lactose, which enhances the creamy texture and sweet, malty flavors reminiscent of burnt sugar, chocolate, and espresso inherent in the brew. Adding malted milk powder to both the cake batter and the glaze further intensifies these flavors—and gives me a good excuse to go shopping for malted milk balls to crush and scatter over the top of the cake after I glaze it.

THE BLACK COW

SERVES 6 TO 8

1 cup [240 ml] milk stout

1 cup [200 g] firmly packed dark brown sugar

⅔ cup [50 g] Dutch-process cocoa powder (see page 13)

½ cup [70 g] malted milk powder

3 eggs

¾ cup [180 ml] canola or vegetable oil

½ cup [120 g] sour cream

2 tsp vanilla extract

1½ cups [210 g] all-purpose flour

1 cup [200 g] granulated sugar

2 tsp baking powder

½ tsp fine sea salt

MALTED CHOCOLATE GLAZE

5 oz [140 g] semisweet chocolate (56 to 60 percent cacao), coarsely chopped, or chocolate chips

½ cup [120 ml] heavy cream

3 Tbsp malted milk powder

1 tsp vanilla extract

6 to 8 malted milk balls, coarsely chopped

Chocolate curls (see page 37) for decorating (optional)

Position a rack in the center of the oven. Preheat the oven to 350°F [180°C]. Coat a 9-by-5-in [23-by-12-cm] metal loaf pan with nonstick cooking spray. Line the pan with an 8½-by-15-in [21.5-by-38-cm] strip of parchment paper so it covers the bottom of the pan and hangs over the long sides.

In a 2- or 3-qt [2- to 2.8-L] saucepan over medium heat, simmer the stout just until hot, but don't let it boil. Whisk in the brown sugar, cocoa powder, and malted milk powder until they dissolve. Remove from the heat and let cool to lukewarm. Whisk in the eggs, oil, sour cream, and vanilla. Set aside.

In a medium bowl, whisk together the flour, granulated sugar, baking powder, and salt.

Using a large balloon whisk, gently whisk the wet ingredients into the dry ingredients, just until they form a thick batter. Be careful not to overmix or the cake will be tough. Using a rubber or silicone spatula, scrape the batter into the prepared pan and smooth the top.

Bake for 55 to 65 minutes, until a wooden skewer inserted into the center of the cake comes out clean.

Transfer the pan to a wire rack and let cool for 10 minutes. Then, grasping the overhanging parchment, lift the loaf out of the pan and set it on the cooling rack. Let cool completely. Discard the parchment paper.

TO MAKE THE GLAZE: Place the chocolate in a small heatproof bowl. In a medium saucepan over medium heat, whisk together the cream and malted milk powder. Heat, stirring occasionally, until the cream is very hot and bubbles start to form around the edges of the pan. Pour the cream over the chocolate. Let sit for 1 minute, and then whisk until smooth. Whisk in the vanilla.

Drizzle the glaze over the top of the cooled loaf, letting it slide down the sides of the cake as it will. Sprinkle the top of the loaf with the chopped malted milk balls, and arrange the chocolate curls in a thin line down the center of the cake. Let the cake sit for at least 1 hour until the glaze is set before slicing. Wrap lightly in plastic wrap and store at room temperature for up to 3 days.

8 oz [230 g] dark chocolate (62 to 70 percent cacao), chopped

1 cup [220 g] unsalted butter

1½ cups [360 ml] brewed coffee

2⅔ cups [530 g] sugar

½ cup [40 g] Dutch-process cocoa powder (see page 13)

¼ cup [60 ml] brandy, cognac, or dark rum

⅓ cup [80 ml] heavy cream

1 Tbsp vanilla extract

3 eggs

2¼ cups [315 g] all-purpose flour

2 tsp baking powder

½ tsp baking soda

1 tsp fine sea salt

CHOCOLATE GLAZE

4 oz [115 g] semisweet chocolate (56 to 60 percent cacao), chopped, or chocolate chips

½ cup [120 ml] heavy cream

1 Tbsp unsalted butter

2 Tbsp mild honey

1 Tbsp brandy, cognac, or coffee liqueur

This dark, dense, intensely chocolate cake is an Australian specialty. Like a cross between an outrageously fudgy brownie and a buttery pound cake, it is often used for wedding cakes because of its durability and great keeping qualities—and the fact that it's best served in modest slivers for all but the most unrepentant chocoholics. Even if you're tempted, don't slice into this cake until it has aged a good 24 hours. Aging allows the texture to soften, and the flavors to ripen and mellow. When properly stored, it stays fresh for many days. It is very important to use a pan that is deep enough to hold all the batter, and make a collar from parchment paper to accommodate the cake's impressive stature as it bakes.

AUSTRALIAN CHOCOLATE MUD CAKE

SERVES 10 TO 12

Position a rack in the center of the oven. Preheat the oven to 300°F [150°C]. Select a 9-in [23-cm] round cake pan or sturdy, leak-proof springform pan with tall sides, at least 3 in [7.5 cm]. Coat the pan with non-stick cooking spray and line the bottom with parchment paper. Cut two parchment strips 5 in [12 cm] wide and 9 in [23 cm] long. Press the strips around the inside of the pan to form a collar, making sure the paper rises up at least 2 in [5 cm] above the top of the pan. The parchment collar will give additional space for the cake batter to rise.

In a 3-qt [2.8-L] saucepan over medium-low heat, combine the chocolate, butter, coffee, sugar, and cocoa powder. Cook, stirring continuously, until the butter and chocolate are completely melted and the sugar is dissolved. Do not let come to a boil.

Remove the pan from the heat and pour the chocolate mixture into a large heat-proof bowl. Let cool for about 10 minutes. Whisk in the brandy, cream, and vanilla. Whisk in the eggs, one at a time, until smooth. Sift in the flour, baking powder, baking soda, and salt and then whisk gently, just until the batter is smooth. Scrape the batter carefully into the prepared pan.

Bake for 1¼ hours. At this point, start testing the cake for doneness; it should be firm and a wooden skewer inserted into the center of the cake should come out clean. The cake will develop a firm top crust; don't let this fool you into thinking the cake is done, as it could still be very liquid in the center. (Mud cake needs to be cooked through—don't be tempted to take this cake out of the oven while the center is still fudgy like a brownie, or it will sink in the center while it is cooling and be too gooey to slice properly.) The cake should be done between 1¼ and 1½ hours.

Transfer the pan to a wire rack and let cool completely, about 3 hours. When the cake is cool, cover tightly with plastic wrap (while still in the pan) and let the cake sit overnight at room temperature. The next day, unwrap and invert the cake onto a cardboard round, serving platter, or cake stand, bottom-side up. Discard all the parchment paper.

TO MAKE THE GLAZE: Place the chocolate in a small heatproof bowl. In a small saucepan over medium heat, bring the cream to a boil. Pour the cream over the chocolate, add the butter and honey, and let sit for about 1 minute. Whisk until smooth, then whisk in the brandy.

Pour the chocolate glaze over the top of the cake, smoothing it with an offset spatula and allowing the excess to drip down the sides of the cake. The cake can be served the day it is glazed, or you can store it in a tightly covered cake carrier at room temperature for up to 3 days.

QUICKIE MILK-CHOCOLATE MOUSSE

12 oz [340 g] milk chocolate, finely chopped

1 cup [240 ml] heavy cream

2 Tbsp chocolate cream liqueur such as Godiva or Mozart

2 Tbsp bourbon, dark rum, or Irish whiskey

BOOZY CHOCOLATE SAUCE

3 to 4 Tbsp sugar

⅓ cup [80 ml] brewed coffee

2 Tbsp unsalted butter

6 oz [170 g] semisweet chocolate (56 to 62 percent cacao), coarsely chopped, or chocolate chips

1 Tbsp Irish whiskey

1 Tbsp dark rum

1 Tbsp chocolate cream liqueur such as Godiva or Mozart

SWEET-AND-SPICY BAR NUTS

1 cup [140 g] unsalted fancy mixed nuts (any mixture of pecan halves, whole almonds, cashews, and pistachios)

1 Tbsp salted butter, melted

2 Tbsp sugar

⅛ tsp cayenne pepper

1 Tbsp Irish whiskey or bourbon

¼ tsp Maldon sea salt for sprinkling

CAKE BATTER

6 oz [170 g] dark chocolate (60 to 62 percent cacao), coarsely chopped

¾ cup [165 g] unsalted butter

¾ cup [150 g] sugar

3 eggs, separated, plus 1 egg yolk

1½ tsp vanilla extract

3 Tbsp Irish whiskey or dark rum, or a combination

⅓ cup [45 g] all-purpose flour

½ tsp fine sea salt

If broken hearts have an edible remedy, this is it—a little chocolate, a little booze, with a few crunchy bar nuts thrown in for good measure. The cake is easy to prepare, but making it is absorbing enough to distract from weightier woes. You can use the combination of spirits I suggest, or just choose one or two of your favorites to make things easier. I love the texture and added zing from the bar nuts, but go ahead and skip them if the added complication causes distress.

HEARTLESS BASTARD BREAK-UP CAKE

SERVES 6 TO 8 (ON A GOOD DAY) / SERVES 1 (ON A BAD DAY)

TO MAKE THE CHOCOLATE MOUSSE: Place the chopped milk chocolate in a medium heatproof bowl. In a medium saucepan over medium-high heat, warm the cream until very hot and small bubbles start to form around the edges of the pan. Just before the cream comes to a boil, pour it over the milk chocolate. Let the mixture sit for 1 minute for the chocolate to soften, then add the chocolate liqueur and bourbon and whisk until smooth. Cover loosely with plastic wrap and refrigerate until very cold, at least 2 hours or up to overnight. If you don't want to wait, pop the chocolate cream into the freezer for 10 to 15 minutes, stirring occasionally, just until very cold (but not frozen.). While the chocolate cream is chilling, make the Boozy Chocolate Sauce, the bar nuts, and the cake.

TO MAKE THE SAUCE: Combine the sugar, coffee, and butter in a medium saucepan over medium-high heat. Stir until the sugar dissolves and the butter melts. Reduce the heat to low and add the chocolate, stirring constantly until the chocolate melts and the mixture is smooth. Stir in the whiskey, rum, and chocolate liqueur and whisk until smooth. Remove from heat and set aside to cool slightly to room temperature.

TO MAKE THE BAR NUTS: Position a rack in the center of the oven. Preheat the oven to 350°F [180°C].

In a medium bowl, toss together the nuts, melted butter, sugar, cayenne, and whiskey. Spread in a single layer on a rimmed baking sheet and toast in the oven for 6 to 8 minutes, stirring once halfway through. Remove the nuts from the oven and transfer to a medium bowl. Crush the Maldon salt with your fingertips, sprinkle over the nuts, and toss to combine.

TO MAKE THE CAKE: Position a rack in the center of the oven. Preheat the oven to 325°F [165°C]. Coat a 9-in [23-cm] round or square cake pan with nonstick cooking spray and line the bottom with parchment paper.

In a medium microwave-safe bowl, combine the chocolate, butter, and sugar. Microwave on high for 1 minute. Stir, then microwave on high for 1 minute longer. Stir until the chocolate and butter are completely melted and the mixture is smooth.

Whisk the egg yolks, one at a time, into the warm chocolate mixture (4 all together). Stir in the vanilla and whiskey. Sift the flour and fine sea salt into the chocolate mixture and gently fold in by hand, using a rubber or silicone spatula, just until smooth. Set aside.

Place the egg whites in a medium bowl. With an electric hand mixer set on low speed, beat the egg whites until opaque and frothy. Increase the mixer speed to medium-high and beat until the egg whites form soft, fluffy peaks and triple in volume, 2 to 3 minutes. With a rubber or silicone spatula, fold one-third of the whites into the chocolate batter to lighten it, and then gently fold in the remaining egg whites, taking care not to deflate them. Scrape the batter into the prepared pan and spread evenly with the spatula.

Bake for 30 to 35 minutes, until a wooden skewer inserted into the center of the cake comes out with moist, fudgy crumbs clinging to it.

TO FINISH THE CAKE: Transfer the cake pan to a wire rack and let cool for 15 minutes. Invert the cake onto a serving plate, discard the parchment paper, and let cool completely. The cake may sink slightly in the center.

Right before serving, whip the chilled chocolate mousse with an electric mixer set on low speed just until it holds soft peaks. Spoon the mousse over the top of the chocolate cake, mounding it in the center. Drizzle with the Boozy Chocolate Sauce, and sprinkle with a few coarsely chopped sweet-and-spicy bar nuts. Devour.

Can't finish it all by yourself? Refrigerate any remaining cake for up to 2 days.

CROWD-PLEASER

When I need an easy, foolproof, and thoroughly addictive chocolate cake in a hurry, or when I want to make an ordinary day feel like a special occasion, this is the chocolate cake I turn to every time. It is luxuriously rich, yet surprisingly light in texture. I've baked easy sheet cakes, cupcakes, and classic double-layer cakes using this batter, and I'm never disappointed. Mayonnaise cakes were popularized in the late 1930s by Hellman's, a well-known maker of mayonnaise, who promoted their product as a more economical substitution for butter and eggs. Since mayonnaise is simply an emulsion of eggs and oil with a dash of vinegar, it works beautifully. Although tasty enough to eat plain or simply sprinkled with confectioners' sugar, I love to slather this cake with Melted Chocolate Bar Frosting, which takes 5 minutes to whip together from pantry staples—all you really need is a bowl, a wooden spoon, and a little muscle.

2 cups [280 g] all-purpose flour

¾ cup [60 g] natural cocoa powder (see page 13)

1 tsp baking powder

¾ tsp baking soda

¼ tsp fine sea salt

2 cups [400 g] granulated sugar

2 eggs

1 cup [240 g] mayonnaise (do not use low-fat)

2 tsp vanilla extract

1 tsp instant espresso powder or instant coffee granules

1⅓ cups [320 ml] boiling water

MELTED CHOCOLATE BAR FROSTING

1 cup [180 g] semisweet chocolate chips

1 cup [180 g] milk chocolate chips

½ cup [110 g] unsalted butter

1 cup [240 g] sour cream

1 tsp vanilla extract

⅛ tsp fine sea salt

2 to 3 cups [240 to 360 g] confectioners' sugar, sifted

OLD-FASHIONED CHOCOLATE MAYONNAISE CAKE WITH MELTED CHOCOLATE BAR FROSTING

SERVES 8 TO 12

Position a rack in the center of the oven. Preheat the oven to 350°F [180°C]. Coat a metal 9-by-13-in [23-by-33-cm] cake pan or two 9-in [23-cm] round cake pans with nonstick cooking spray. If using 9-in [23-cm] round pans, line the bottoms with parchment paper.

In a medium bowl, sift together the flour, cocoa powder, baking powder, baking soda, and salt. Set aside.

In the bowl of a stand mixer fitted with the paddle attachment, beat the granulated sugar and eggs together at medium-high speed until light and fluffy, 3 to 4 minutes. Beat in the mayonnaise and vanilla until smooth.

Continued

Decrease the mixer speed to low and beat in half of the dry ingredients just until combined. Stop the mixer and scrape down the sides of the bowl.

In a small bowl, stir together the espresso powder and boiling water. Add half of the espresso mixture to the batter and beat on low speed just until the batter is smooth, 5 to 10 seconds. Add the remaining dry ingredients and beat just until combined. Beat in the remaining espresso and beat just until smooth. The batter will be somewhat thin. Scrape the batter into the prepared pan(s) and spread evenly with a spatula.

Bake for 22 to 25 minutes, until a wooden skewer inserted into the center of the cake comes out clean. Transfer the pan(s) to a wire rack and let cool completely, about 30 minutes.

TO MAKE THE FROSTING: In a large microwave-safe bowl, combine the semi-sweet and milk chocolate chips with the butter. Microwave on high for 1 minute. Stir together until the butter and choco-lates are completely melted and smooth. If not completely melted after 1 minute, heat again in 15-second increments, stirring between each, until smooth and shiny. Using a large balloon whisk or a wooden spoon, stir in the sour cream, vanilla, and salt. Beat in 2 cups [240 g] of the confectioners' sugar, just until smooth and spreadable. Let the frosting set for a few minutes at room temperature, as it will firm up a little as it cools. If a thicker, sweeter, frosting is desired, beat in the remaining 1 cup [120 g] confectioners' sugar.

TO FINISH THE CAKE: For a sheet cake, leave the cake in the pan and spread the top with the frosting. Cut into squares and serve. If making a layer cake, place one layer on a cake plate or cake stand and spread with one-third of the frosting. Top with a second layer and spread the remaining frosting evenly over the top and around the sides of the cake. Cut into wedges and serve. To store, cover the sheet cake with plastic wrap or aluminum foil. Store the layer cake in a tightly cov-ered cake carrier. Both will keep at room temperature for up to 3 days.

Chocolate and coffee are a happy combination that never, ever gets old. Here layers of rich chocolate cake are sandwiched with a mild, simple-to-make milk chocolate cream spiked with a shot of espresso. *Stracciatella* means "little rags" or "shreds" in Italian—in this case, referring to the little grated pieces of semisweet chocolate swirled through the delicate Swiss meringue buttercream.

SHOT IN THE DARK

SERVES 8 TO 10

2 cups [280 g] all-purpose flour

2¼ tsp baking powder

1 tsp fine sea salt

1 cup [80 g] Dutch-process cocoa powder (see page 13)

1¼ cups [300 ml] hot, strong brewed coffee

1¼ cups [275 g] unsalted butter, at room temperature

2⅓ cups [465 g] sugar

3 eggs, plus 2 egg yolks, at room temperature

2 tsp vanilla extract

1 cup [240 g] sour cream, at room temperature

MILK CHOCOLATE–ESPRESSO GANACHE

1 lb [455 g] milk chocolate, coarsely chopped

1 cup [240 ml] heavy cream

¼ cup [60 ml] brewed espresso

1 tsp vanilla extract

ESPRESSO–STRACCIATELLA BUTTERCREAM

1 to 2 tsp instant espresso powder

1 Tbsp vanilla bean paste

1 tsp hot water

8 egg whites

2 cups [400 g] sugar

3 cups [660 g] unsalted butter, at very soft room temperature

4 oz [115 g] semisweet chocolate

Position a rack in the center of the oven. Preheat the oven to 350°F [180°C]. Coat three 8-in [23-cm] round cake pans with nonstick cooking spray and line the bottoms with parchment paper.

In a medium bowl, sift together the flour, baking powder, and salt. Set aside.

In another medium bowl, whisk together the cocoa powder and hot coffee until smooth. Set aside.

In a stand mixer fitted with the paddle attachment, beat the butter and sugar together on medium-high speed until light and fluffy, 3 to 4 minutes. Add the whole eggs, one at a time, beating well after each addition. Scrape down the sides of the bowl with a rubber or silicone spatula and beat in the egg yolks, one at a time. Beat in the cooled cocoa-coffee paste and the vanilla, just until smooth.

On low speed, beat half of the dry ingredients into the batter just until smooth and combined, 10 to 15 seconds. Scrape down the sides of the bowl and beat in the sour cream, just until combined,

10 to 15 seconds. Beat in the remaining dry ingredients. Divide the batter evenly between the prepared cake pans and smooth the tops with an offset spatula.

Bake for 22 to 25 minutes, until a wooden skewer inserted into the center of each cake comes out clean.

Transfer the pans to wire racks and let cool for 10 minutes. Invert the cakes onto the racks, discard the parchment paper, and let cool completely.

TO MAKE THE MILK CHOCOLATE–ESPRESSO GANACHE: Place the chopped milk chocolate in a medium heatproof bowl. In a small saucepan over medium heat, combine the cream and espresso and bring to a simmer. When bubbles form around the edges of the pan and the cream is very hot but is just starting to boil, remove from the heat and pour over the chocolate. Let sit for 1 to 2 minutes to soften, then whisk until smooth. Let cool to room temperature, cover loosely with plastic wrap, and refrigerate for at least 2 hours, or until the ganache reaches spreading consistency.

Continued

TO MAKE THE BUTTERCREAM: In a small bowl, dissolve 1 tsp of the instant espresso powder and the vanilla bean paste in the hot water and set aside.

Fill a large sauté pan or skillet with water and bring to a simmer over medium heat. Combine the egg whites and sugar in the bowl of a stand mixer and place the bowl in the pan of simmering water. By hand, using a large balloon whisk, beat the egg whites and sugar together constantly until the sugar is completely dissolved and is no longer gritty, and the mixture is very thick and frothy and hot to the touch (it should register between 120° and 140°F [48° and 60°C] on an instant-read candy thermometer), 3 to 5 minutes.

Remove the bowl from the simmering water. Using the stand mixer fitted with the whisk attachment, beat the egg white mixture at high speed until it triples in volume, forming stiff, glossy peaks. Beat until the bottom of the bowl is completely cool to the touch, 10 to 13 minutes.

Gradually beat in the softened butter, 2 Tbsp at a time, beating well after each addition. Don't start to panic if the buttercream starts to liquefy or look curdled as you beat in the butter. It will magically emulsify into a smooth, silky frosting by the time the last bit of butter is incorporated. Continue beating, and slowly drizzle in the vanilla-espresso paste. Taste the buttercream. If a stronger espresso flavor is desired, dissolve the remaining 1 tsp instant espresso in 1 tsp hot water and beat into the buttercream.

Using the large holes of a box grater or with a coarse Microplane zester, grate the chocolate. Fold the grated chocolate into the buttercream by hand, using a rubber or silicone spatula.

TO FINISH THE CAKE: Place one cake layer on a cardboard cake round bottom-side up. Spread the cake with 1 cup of the ganache and top with the second cake layer. Spread the second layer with 1 cup of ganache and top with the third cake layer. Refrigerate for 30 minutes to set the ganache.

Spread the top and sides of the cake with a thin layer of buttercream as a crumb coat (see page 21). Refrigerate for 15 minutes to set. Spread the remaining buttercream over the top and sides of the cake, smoothing it with an offset spatula.

The cake can be frosted and refrigerated in a covered cake carrier up to 2 days. Let the cake come to room temperature 1 to 2 hours before slicing and serving.

Intense, boozy, deadly. This layer cake isn't a blushing flower, and to achieve its knockout chocolate flavor and color I combine natural and Dutch-process cocoa powders with a little splash of black cocoa. Never heard of it? Black cocoa powder is an ultra-Dutched cocoa with a rich, mellow chocolate flavor and deep, dark color that is almost as black as its name (see page 34). If you have ever wondered where Oreo cookies get their inky hue, it's from black cocoa powder. Not commonly stocked in supermarkets, black cocoa is worth tracking down. I buy it from King Arthur Flour (www.kingarthurflour.com). But if you can't find it, simply increase the amount of regular Dutch-process cocoa called for in this recipe from 6 Tbsp to 8 Tbsp. The combination of different cocoas delivers a fierce chocolate flavor that holds its own against a generous tipple of Irish whiskey in both the cake and the elegant, dark chocolate ganache. If possible, make the ganache a day in advance and let it sit at room temperature to achieve the best spreading consistency.

BLACK IRISH CHOCOLATE-WHISKEY CAKE

SERVES 8 TO 10

2¼ cups [315 g] all-purpose flour

2 tsp baking powder

1 tsp baking soda

1 tsp fine sea salt

½ cup [40 g] natural cocoa powder (see page 13)

⅓ cup [25 g] Dutch-process cocoa powder (see page 13)

2 Tbsp black cocoa (see headnote)

3 oz [85 g] semisweet chocolate, finely chopped

1 cup [240 ml] very hot coffee

⅓ cup [80 ml] Irish whiskey

3 eggs

1½ cups [300 g] granulated sugar

1 cup [200 g] firmly packed dark brown sugar

2 tsp vanilla extract

¾ cup [180 ml] vegetable oil

1¼ cups [300 ml] buttermilk

IRISH WHISKEY CHOCOLATE GANACHE

1½ lb [680 g] semisweet chocolate (56 to 60 percent cacao), chopped

2¼ cups [540 ml] heavy cream

½ tsp instant espresso powder

3 Tbsp unsalted butter, at room temperature

3 Tbsp Golden Syrup (see page 17) or light corn syrup

¼ cup [60 ml] Irish whiskey

Position a rack in the center of the oven. Preheat the oven to 350°F [180°C]. Coat two 9-in [23-cm] round cake pans with non-stick cooking spray and line the bottoms with parchment paper.

In a medium bowl, sift together the flour, baking powder, baking soda, and salt. Set aside.

In a separate medium bowl, whisk together all three cocoa powders, the chocolate, hot coffee, and whiskey until smooth. Let cool to lukewarm.

In the bowl of a stand mixer fitted with the paddle attachment, beat together the eggs, granulated sugar, and brown sugar on medium speed until light and fluffy, 3 to 4 minutes. Beat in the vanilla. Gradually add the vegetable oil in a thin, steady stream, beating continuously. Add the cocoa mixture, beating until combined. Scrape down the sides of the bowl.

On low speed, beat one-third of the dry ingredients into the batter, just until combined, 15 to 20 seconds. Beat in half of the buttermilk. When combined, add another one-third of the dry ingredients, mixing just until no white streaks remain, 10 to 15 seconds. Add the rest of the buttermilk, then the remaining flour mixture, beating just until smooth. Be careful not to over-beat the batter, as this will toughen the cake. Divide the batter evenly between the prepared pans, smoothing the tops with a spatula.

Bake for 25 to 30 minutes, or just until a wooden skewer inserted into the center of each cake comes out clean.

Transfer the pans to wire racks and let cool for 10 minutes. Invert the cakes onto the racks, discarding the parchment paper, and let cool completely.

TO MAKE THE GANACHE: Place the chocolate in a medium heatproof bowl. In a small saucepan over medium-high heat, combine the cream and espresso powder. Bring just to a boil, stirring to dissolve the espresso powder. Pour the hot cream over the chocolate and let stand for 1 to 2 minutes to soften. Add the butter, golden syrup, and whiskey and whisk until the butter is melted and the ganache is smooth. For the perfect spreading consis-tency, let the ganache stand for 12 to 24 hours at room temperature to cool and thicken.

TO FINISH THE CAKE: Split each cake layer in half horizontally (see page 21), creating four layers. Place one of the layers on a cardboard cake round, cake plate, or cake stand, cut-side up, and spread with about one-fourth of the ganache. Top with the second cake layer, cut-side down, and spread with another one-fourth of the ganache. Place the third layer, cut-side up, and spread with

another one-fourth of the ganache. Top with the final cake layer, cut-side down. Refrigerate the cake for 30 minutes to set the filling. Using an offset spatula, frost the top and sides of the cake with the remaining ganache.

Store in a covered cake carrier at room temperature up to 1 day before serving, or refrigerate for up to 2 days. Allow the cake to come to room temperature for 1 to 2 hours before slicing.

81

2¾ cups [385 g] all-purpose flour

1 cup [80 g] natural cocoa powder (see page 13)

1½ tsp baking powder

1½ tsp baking soda

1 tsp fine sea salt

2 cups [400 g] granulated sugar

1½ cups [300 g] firmly packed dark brown sugar

1 Tbsp instant espresso powder

1 Tbsp vanilla extract

1 cup [240 g] sour cream

3 eggs

1¼ cups [300 ml] canola or vegetable oil

1⅓ cups [320 ml] boiling water

CHOCOLATE—PEANUT BUTTER PUDDING

½ cup [100 g] sugar

3 Tbsp cornstarch

⅛ tsp fine sea salt

3 Tbsp natural or Dutch-process cocoa powder (see page 13)

2½ cups [600 ml] half-and-half or whole milk, or a mixture of the two

4 egg yolks

1 tsp vanilla extract

¼ cup [65 g] creamy peanut butter

½ cup [85 g] semisweet chocolate chips

CREAMY PEANUT BUTTER FROSTING

1½ cups [330 g] unsalted butter, at room temperature

1 cup [260 g] creamy peanut butter

4 cups [480 g] confectioners' sugar, sifted

1 tsp vanilla extract

3 to 4 Tbsp cold milk

CARAMEL SAUCE

1 cup [200 g] sugar

2 Tbsp water

¾ cup [180 ml] heavy cream

3 Tbsp unsalted butter

1 tsp vanilla extract

¼ tsp fine sea salt

CHOCOLATE GLAZE

6 oz [170 g] semisweet chocolate, chopped, or semisweet chocolate chips

2 Tbsp coconut oil, melted then measured again

2 Tbsp Golden Syrup (see page 17) or light corn syrup

¼ to ⅓ cup [35 to 45 g] salted peanut halves

Like a candy bar in cake form, this large and impressive dessert has three chocolate cake layers stuffed with homemade chocolate–peanut butter pudding and frosted with a fluffy, creamy peanut-butter frosting. Not one, but two gooey, drippy glazes are poured over the top to cascade down the sides: a thick caramel sauce topped by a dark, shining chocolate cap. A handful of salted peanuts sprinkled on top of the cake makes a fun and simple garnish that hints at the flavors within. The pudding can be made a day or two ahead, giving it plenty of time to firm up before you assemble the cake.

CHOCOLATE– PEANUT BUTTER BLACKOUT CAKE

SERVES 8 TO 10

Position a rack in the center of the oven. Preheat the oven to 350°F [180°C]. Coat three 9-in [23-cm] round cake pans with nonstick cooking spray and line the bottoms with parchment paper.

In a large bowl, sift together the flour, cocoa powder, baking powder, baking soda, and salt. Set aside.

In the bowl of stand mixer fitted with the paddle attachment, beat together the granulated sugar, brown sugar, espresso powder, vanilla, sour cream, and eggs on low speed until smooth. With the mixer running, drizzle in the oil in a steady stream and beat for a few seconds until creamy and well combined.

With the mixer still on low speed, beat the dry ingredients into the wet ingredients in three additions, beating 10 to 15 seconds after each, just until smooth. Stop the mixer and scrape down the sides of the bowl. Add the boiling water to the batter and beat on low speed, 10 to 15 seconds, just until the batter is smooth. Be careful not to splash! The batter will be fairly thin. Divide the batter evenly between the three prepared pans, smoothing the tops with a spatula. Bake for 25 to 30 minutes, until a wooden skewer inserted into the center of each cake comes out clean.

Transfer the pans to wire racks and let cool for 10 minutes. Invert the cakes onto the racks, discard the parchment paper, and let cool completely.

Continued

TO MAKE THE PUDDING: In a medium saucepan, sift together the sugar, cornstarch, salt, and cocoa powder. Slowly whisk in the half-and-half and then the egg yolks, one at a time, until smooth.

Cook over medium heat, whisking continuously, until the pudding starts to thicken and comes to a gentle boil, and large bubbles form and plop on the surface like slowly bubbling hot lava. Decrease the heat to low and continue cooking, still whisking, 1 to 2 minutes longer, until the pudding is thick enough to coat the back of a spoon.

Remove the pudding from the heat and stir in the vanilla, peanut butter, and chocolate chips. Stir until the chocolate is melted and the pudding is smooth. Pour into a bowl and cover with plastic wrap, pressing it onto the surface of the pudding to prevent a skin from forming. Refrigerate until cold and very firm, at least 4 hours and preferably overnight.

TO MAKE THE FROSTING: In a stand mixer fitted with the paddle attachment, beat the butter and peanut butter together on medium speed until creamy and fluffy. Add the confectioners' sugar and beat on low speed until crumbly. Add the vanilla, increase the speed to medium-high, and continue beating until thick and creamy. Add the milk, 1 Tbsp at a time, and continue beating until fluffy and spreadable, adding more milk if necessary, a few teaspoons at a time, to reach the proper consistency.

Place one cake layer on a cardboard cake round, bottom-side up. Fit a large disposable piping bag with a large round tip and fill with one-fourth of the peanut butter frosting. Pipe a rope of peanut butter frosting around the edge of the cake to form a dam. Spread half of the cold pudding evenly inside the frosting dam, and top with the next cake layer. Pipe another frosting dam around the edge of the second cake layer and fill with the rest of the pudding. Top with the final cake layer. Refrigerate for 15 to 20 minutes to allow the filling to firm up a bit before you continue.

Spread the top and sides of the chilled cake with a thin layer of peanut butter frosting to form a crumb coat (see page 21). Refrigerate for about 30 minutes, until the frosting is very firm. Spread the remaining peanut butter frosting over the top and sides of the cake, smoothing it evenly with an offset spatula. Refrigerate until very cold and firm, at least 1 hour or overnight.

TO MAKE THE CARAMEL SAUCE: While the cake is chilling, in a heavy 2-qt [2-L] stainless-steel saucepan over medium heat, combine the sugar and water. Cook, gently swirling the pan occasionally (do not stir), until the sugar dissolves and starts to caramelize. Increase the heat to high and boil until the syrup turns a deep golden amber (the color of an old penny), 4 to 6 minutes. Immediately remove the pan from the heat and pour in the cream. Using a long-handled wooden spoon, stir until smooth. Be careful, as the cream will bubble vigorously when it hits the hot caramel. Simmer over low heat, stirring occasionally, for 2 to 3 minutes, until the caramel thickens slightly. Remove from the heat and add the butter, vanilla, and salt, stirring until smooth. Set aside and let cool until the sauce is lukewarm but still pourable.

Place the frosted cake on a wire rack over a rimmed baking sheet. Pour the caramel sauce over the top of the cake, smoothing with a metal offset spatula and spreading so it completely covers the top of the cake and drips generously down the sides. Refrigerate for 20 to 30 minutes to set until very firm.

TO MAKE THE CHOCOLATE GLAZE: Place the chocolate, coconut oil, and golden syrup in a microwave-safe bowl and microwave on high for 1 minute. Stir until smooth. If the chocolate isn't completely melted, heat in 15-second increments, stirring after each, until smooth.

Pour the warm chocolate glaze over the cake, again covering the top completely, smoothing the glaze with a metal offset spatula, and letting the excess drip down the sides of the cake. Leave the peanut butter frosting slightly exposed. While the chocolate glaze is still soft, sprinkle the salted peanut halves around the top of the cake. Refrigerate until firm.

Transfer the cake to a cake stand and let it sit at room temperature for 1 to 2 hours before slicing and serving. Cover any leftover cake loosely with plastic wrap and store in the refrigerator for up to 2 days.

My daughter Sophia never met a chocolate cake she didn't fall madly in love with, so a special occasion like her thirteenth birthday demanded a real show-stopper. This extravagant confection features rich chocolate cake, gooey caramel, and a pillowy layer of homemade marshmallow. A mousse-like buttercream and real Belgian chocolate sprinkles push this cake over the top. Save time (and your sanity) by preparing the marshmallow layer up to one week in advance.

THE SCOTCHMALLOW

SERVES 8 TO 10

Position a rack in the center of the oven. Preheat the oven to 350°F [180°C]. Coat two 9-in [23-cm] round cake pans with nonstick cooking spray. Line the bottoms with parchment paper.

In a medium bowl, sift together the flour, baking powder, baking soda, and salt. Set aside.

In a heatproof bowl, combine the cocoa powder, espresso powder, and chocolate. Pour in the boiling water and stir until the chocolate is melted and the mixture is smooth. Stir in the vanilla and buttermilk. Set aside and let cool.

In the bowl of a stand mixer fitted with the paddle attachment, beat the butter and oil on medium speed until creamy. Add both the sugars and continue beating until light and fluffy, 3 to 4 minutes. Add the eggs, one at a time, beating well after each addition. Beat in the egg yolks. Scrape down the sides of the bowl.

Add one-third of the dry ingredients to the batter and beat at low speed for 10 to 15 seconds, just until combined. Beat in half of the chocolate mixture for a few

seconds, just to combine. Beat in another one-third of the dry ingredients, followed by the remaining chocolate mixture. Scrape down the sides of the bowl, and finally beat in the remaining one-third of the dry ingredients at low speed just until no streaks of flour remain, about 10 to 15 seconds. Divide the batter evenly between the prepared pans and spread the tops smooth with a spatula.

Bake for 25 to 30 minutes, until a wooden skewer inserted into the center of each cake comes out clean. Transfer the pans to wire racks and let cool for 10 minutes. Invert the cakes onto the racks, discard the parchment paper, and let cool completely.

TO MAKE THE BUTTERCREAM: Fill a large sauté pan with water and bring to a simmer over medium heat. Combine the eggs and sugar in the bowl of a stand mixer. Set the bowl in the pan of simmering water. By hand, using a large balloon whisk, vigorously beat the eggs and sugar until the sugar is completely dissolved and the mixture is thick, fluffy, and very hot, 3 to 4 minutes. Use an instant-read candy ther-mometer to check the temperature of the

2½ cups [350 g] all-purpose flour

2 tsp baking powder

½ tsp baking soda

¾ tsp fine sea salt

⅔ cup [50 g] Dutch-process cocoa powder (see page 13)

1 tsp instant espresso powder

3 oz [85 g] semisweet chocolate, finely chopped

1 cup [240 ml] boiling water

2 tsp vanilla extract

1 cup [240 ml] buttermilk

½ cup [110 g] unsalted butter, at room temperature

½ cup [120 ml] canola or vegetable oil

1½ cups [300 g] granulated sugar

1 cup [200 g] firmly packed dark brown sugar

3 eggs, plus 2 egg yolks, at room temperature

CHOCOLATE SILK BUTTERCREAM

6 eggs

1½ cups [300 g] granulated sugar

1 tsp vanilla extract

⅛ tsp fine sea salt

3 cups [660 g] unsalted butter, at room temperature

12 oz [340 g] semisweet chocolate (56 to 60 percent cacao), melted and cooled

CARAMEL DRIZZLE

1 cup [200 g] granulated sugar

2 Tbsp water

¾ cup [180 ml] heavy cream

1 tsp vanilla extract

¼ tsp fine sea salt

MARSHMALLOW LAYER

Cornstarch for dusting

1 cup [240 ml] cold water

3 Tbsp unflavored granulated gelatin

2 cups [400 g] granulated sugar

¾ cup [180 ml] light corn syrup

¼ tsp fine sea salt

1½ tsp vanilla extract

Confectioners' sugar for dusting

1 cup [180 g] Belgian chocolate sprinkles (optional)

Continued

whipped eggs and sugar; it should register between 120° and 140°F [48° and 60°C].

Remove the bowl from the hot water and return to the stand mixer. Using the whisk attachment, beat the eggs at high speed until they are tripled in volume, form stiff peaks, and the bottom of the bowl is completely cool to the touch, 10 to 13 minutes. Beat in the vanilla and salt.

With the mixer still on high speed, add the softened butter, 2 Tbsp at a time, adding more butter only as each addition is fully incorporated. Don't panic if the buttercream looks too liquid or starts to curdle as you add the butter. It will magically emulsify into a smooth, creamy frosting by the time the last bit of butter is beaten in. Hold your breath and keep beating. When the buttercream is smooth and all the butter has been incorporated, turn off the mixer and, using a rubber or silicone spatula, carefully fold in the cooled melted chocolate by hand.

TO MAKE THE CARAMEL DRIZZLE: In a large, heavy saucepan over medium-high heat, combine the sugar and water. Cook, without stirring but swirling the pan occasionally, until the sugar is completely dissolved. Bring to a boil and cook, undisturbed, until the syrup turns a deep amber (the color of an old penny), 4 to 6 minutes. Immediately remove the pan from the heat and, using a long-handled wooden spoon, stir in the cream. Be careful, as the cream will bubble vigorously when it hits the hot caramel. Return the pan to medium-low heat and stir the sauce until it is thick and creamy, 2 to 3 minutes. Remove from the heat, stir in the vanilla and salt, and let cool.

TO MAKE THE MARSHMALLOW LAYER: At least 1 day (and up to 1 week) ahead, coat a 9-in [23-cm] round cake pan with nonstick cooking spray and dust liberally with cornstarch. Set aside.

Pour ½ cup [120 ml] of the cold water into the bowl of a stand mixer and sprinkle with the gelatin. Allow the gelatin to absorb the water, 15 to 20 minutes.

In a large saucepan over medium heat, combine the remaining ½ cup [120 ml] water, the granulated sugar, corn syrup, and salt. Heat, swirling the pan occasionally, until the sugar dissolves. Increase the heat to high and let the syrup come to a boil. Cook, without stirring, until it reaches 240°F [115°C] on an instant-read candy thermometer. Do not allow the syrup to go past 244°F [117°C] or the marshmallow will be tough and rubbery.

With the mixer on low, beat the syrup into the gelatin, using the whisk attachment of the mixer. Increase the mixer speed to high and continue beating until the marshmallow is thick, fluffy, and very white but still warm, 10 to 13 minutes. Beat in the vanilla.

Scrape the marshmallow into the prepared pan, smooth the surface with a spatula, and dust with confectioners' sugar. Let the marshmallow stand, uncovered, for 8 to 12 hours to firm up. Turn the marshmallow onto a piece of parchment paper lightly dusted with confectioners' sugar. Brush away any excess cornstarch. (Store the marshmallow layer in a covered container or large, self-sealing plastic bag for up to 1 week.)

TO FINISH THE CAKE: Place one cake layer, bottom-side up, on a cardboard cake round. Transfer 1 rounded cup [about 300 g] buttercream into a disposable piping bag fitted with a large round or star tip and set aside.

Spread the surface of the cake with 1 rounded cup buttercream. Drizzle with approximately ⅓ cup [80 ml] of the cool caramel drizzle. Top with the second layer of cake. Spread with another 1 cup of buttercream and drizzle with another ⅓ cup of the caramel.

Use a pastry brush to brush any remnants of cornstarch and confectioners' sugar from the marshmallow layer and place it on top of the cake. Press down gently to make sure it has adhered to the caramel and buttercream. Frost the sides of the cake with a thin coat of buttercream to form a crumb coat (see page 21), and refrigerate for 15 to 20 minutes to firm up. With the remaining buttercream, frost the top and sides of the cake, completely covering the cake and marshmallow. If desired, press Belgian chocolate sprinkles on the sides of the cake (place the cake and turntable, if using, on a rimmed baking sheet to catch any errant sprinkles). Press the sprinkles by the handful around the sides of the cake, slowly spinning the turntable as you go (if you're using a turntable) until the cake is completely encrusted.

Spoon approximately ½ cup [120 ml] of the lukewarm caramel over the top of the cake, letting it drizzle down the sides. With the reserved buttercream, pipe a decorative pattern over the top of the cake. Serve at room temperature.

Refrigerate in a cake carrier for up to 2 days. Let the cake come to room temperature for 1 to 2 hours before serving.

CARAMEL &
BUTTERSCOTCH

One of my secret vices as a child was sneaking into the pantry and rummaging for old boxes of brown sugar. I looked for poorly sealed open boxes where the moist sugar had hardened into solid rocks of grainy candy. I would break off a chunk and let it dissolve on my tongue, relishing the rich butterscotch sweetness—and the furtive guilty pleasure—with the same intensity. I still find the flavors of butterscotch and caramel—and their Latin cousin dulce de leche—enchanting. Simultaneously smooth and sweet, buttery and smoky, their character is complex and defies simple description. Rumpelstiltskin, that fairy-tale alchemist who could spin common straw into gold, would understand the allure, and the kitchen magic required, for turning plain and simple sugar into caramel gold.

CARAMEL BASICS

Caramel, butterscotch, and dulce de leche may look the same, and they may share many of the same characteristics, but they really are very different. Butterscotch is hearty and gutsy. It's cheerful and a little old-fashioned, with a robust, down-to-earth, buttery sweetness. To make butterscotch, brown sugar and butter are melted together and cooked to a gooey, golden toffee. With a little cream and a judicious pinch of salt stirred in, the flavor blooms. Butterscotch isn't very fiddly or temperature sensitive—and a little corn syrup stirred into the sauce will combat any graininess as the butterscotch cools. All in all, it's pretty simple.

Caramel, on the other hand, is more complex—smoky and seductive, even a bit dangerous. It's a little demanding and slightly temperamental. When you are concentrating on caramel, you can have eyes for nothing else. The primary ingredient in caramel is granulated pure cane sugar. To make it, sugar is cooked until it melts, the heat transforming it from a pale golden syrup to a deeper amber, the color of a well-worn penny. When the aroma of ever-so-slightly burnt sugar tickles your nose, whisk in heavy cream. Good caramel—whether in syrup, sauce or candy form—captures the perfect balance of sweetness and smoke, with just a hint of bitterness for added complexity.

DON'T FEAR THE CANDY THERMOMETER

Many people see the words "candy thermometer" in a recipe and immediately turn the page, judging the recipe too complicated for them to attempt. Actually, using a candy thermometer when making sugar syrups for caramel, marshmallows, and French or Italian meringue buttercream takes all the guesswork and decision making out of your hands. No more worrying if you cooked the caramel for 3 minutes—or was it five? No more wondering what exactly the difference is between the "thread stage" and the "soft-ball stage." Candy thermometers make your life easy.

Candy thermometers are fairly inexpensive gadgets to add to your *batterie de cuisine*, and they are small enough to store easily in the most overstuffed kitchen drawer. The least expensive models use a glass tube in a metal body with a clip that attaches to the side of the pot. The mercury bulb should sit low enough to read the temperature of the liquid it is immersed in without touching the bottom of the saucepan. The thermometer should read a range of temperatures from at least 100° to 400°F [38° to 204°C].

More expensive, battery-operated digital thermometers have an even greater range—from 52° to 572°F [11° to 290°C]. They are fast, very accurate, and easy to read—a good investment if you become an aficionado of homemade caramel and marshmallows.

THE COLD WATER TEST

As the sugar syrup cooks, you can drip a little periodically into ice water to show what the consistency will be when it cools.

Thread Stage (215° to 235°F [106° to 112°C]): Sugar syrup. Does not harden when cooled.

Soft-Ball Stage (235° to 240°F [112° to 116°C]): Forms a sticky, squishy ball, easily flattened when pressed with fingers. (Fudge, fondant, penuche, pralines, Italian meringue, caramel icing.)

Firm-Ball Stage (242° to 250°F [118°C to 120°C]): Immediately forms a soft, malleable ball that will just barely hold its shape. (Caramels, marshmallow, divinity.)

Hard-Ball Stage (250° to 265°F [121° to 130°C]): Forms a firm ball that holds its shape but is not hard. (Nougat, taffy, gummie candy.)

Soft-Crack Stage (270° to 290°F [132° to 143°C]): Syrup separates into stretchy, firm strands. (Butterscotch, toffee.)

Hard-Crack Stage (300° to 310°F [149° to 154°C]): Strands solidify into hard brittle threads. (Peanut brittle, hard candy, lollipops.)

Light Caramel Stage (320° to 335°F [160° to 170°C]): Golden, honey-colored light and brittle coating. (Candy apples.)

Dark Caramel Stage (345° to 350°F [174° to 175°C]): Dark caramel coating, a deep reddish color. (Starter syrup for caramel sauce, spun sugar.)

MAKING CARAMEL

Making caramel feels like a magic trick. Take one simple ingredient—granulated sugar—apply a little heat, and poof! It transforms into liquid gold.

Dry Method: The dry method for making caramel works best in small batches. Place sugar in a stainless-steel saucepan and cook over low heat, stirring occasionally with a fork, until the sugar melts and starts to turn color. As the sugar cooks, it will caramelize and become fragrant, turning from a pale golden color to dark amber in a matter of seconds. You have to watch the caramel carefully because it can start to burn and smoke very quickly, and burnt caramel cannot be saved. When the caramel reaches the correct well-worn copper penny color (between 345° and 348°F [174° and 176°C] on a candy thermometer), remove it from the heat and stir in cream or other liquid to stop the sugar from cooking any further.

Wet Method: Sugar is mixed with a little water until it forms a sandy paste. A little cream of tartar or lemon juice can be added to prevent recrystallization of any of the sugar crystals. The sugar is allowed to dissolve, completely undisturbed, over medium heat. Once it comes to a boil, it isn't stirred, merely swirled in the pan to ensure even caramelization. As with the dry method, once the sugar reaches the proper dark amber color, remove it from the heat and stir in cream or water to stop it from cooking any further.

DIY DULCE DE LECHE

Dulce de leche, beloved for its mild, comforting sweetness, literally translated as "milk jam" or "milk sweet," is the third leg in the sticky-gooey trifecta that includes butterscotch and caramel.

You can buy dulce de leche, but it's so easy to make yourself, why not give it a try? You can store it in the refrigerator in a covered container for up to 3 weeks.

Oven Method: Position a rack in the center of the oven. Preheat the oven to 400°F [200°C]. Pour two 14-oz [400-g] cans sweetened condensed milk into a 2½-qt [2.4-L] ovenproof bowl. Stir in 2 tsp vanilla extract and a pinch of salt. Cover tightly with aluminum foil and place the bowl in a roasting pan. Fill the roasting pan with boiling water until it reaches halfway up the sides of the bowl. Cook for about 2 hours, until the condensed milk is thick, jammy, and a deep, golden brown. Keep an eye on the water level in the roasting pan, filling it with more boiling water as needed. Set aside to cool.

Microwave Method: Pour two 14-oz [400-g] cans sweetened condensed milk into a 2½-qt [2.4-L] ovenproof bowl. Stir in 3 Tbsp water, 2 tsp vanilla extract, and a pinch of salt. Cover the bowl with a paper towel (to prevent splattering) and microwave on 50 percent power for 5 minutes. Remove from the microwave and stir. Cook on 50 percent power for an additional 10 to 15 minutes, stirring every 2 to 3 minutes, until the condensed milk is thick, gooey, and golden brown. Set aside to cool.

Stovetop Method (easy but daring): Remove the labels from two 14-oz [400-g] cans of sweetened condensed milk. Place the cans on their sides in a large stockpot and fill with water so that the cans are well submerged in water. Bring the water to a boil and cook, uncovered, making sure that the cans remain covered at all times with boiling water. I can't emphasize enough how important it is to keep the cans covered with plenty of water as the milk cooks. If the water level drops below the cans, there is a risk that the cans can burst. Big. Scary. Mess. I keep a teakettle filled with boiling water to top off the stockpot as needed. After 2½ to 3 hours, remove the stockpot from the heat and let the cans cool completely in the water. Once the cans are cool, empty the dulce de leche into a covered container and store in the refrigerator for up to 3 weeks.

1½ cups [210 g] all-purpose flour

1 tsp baking powder

¾ tsp fine sea salt

½ cup [60 g] very finely chopped pecans, toasted (see page 16)

½ cup plus 6 Tbsp [200 g] unsalted butter, at room temperature

4 oz [120 g] cream cheese, at room temperature

1 cup [200 g] granulated sugar

⅔ cup [130 g] firmly packed dark brown sugar

4 eggs, at room temperature

1 Tbsp vanilla bean paste

2 Tbsp bourbon

BOURBON PECAN-PRALINE GLAZE

¼ cup [50 g] firmly packed dark brown sugar

3 Tbsp unsalted butter

2 Tbsp Golden Syrup (see page 17) or light corn syrup

1 Tbsp bourbon

⅛ tsp fine sea salt

¼ cup [60 ml] heavy cream

½ cup [60 g] confectioners' sugar, sifted

½ tsp vanilla extract

½ cup [60 g] coarsely chopped pecans, toasted and cooled (see page 16)

Pound cake is not a foolproof cure for loneliness, but it helps. One day, as a young navy wife, I sat sniffling at an impromptu potluck in the kitchen of a new friend. She had weathered many more long deployments than I had, and her eyes were dry. She patted my shoulder and handed me a thick slice of cream-cheese pound cake, heavy for its size, with a dense, buttery crumb and a golden, chewy crust. For a moment, I forgot my troubles and focused on the sheer pleasure of eating it. Cream-cheese pound cake is rich, with a wonderful vanilla aroma—here made extra special with a fudgy pecan-praline glaze drizzled over the top.

PECAN-PRALINE CREAM-CHEESE POUND CAKE

SERVES 6 TO 8

Position a rack in the center of the oven. Preheat the oven to 325°F [165°C]. Coat a 9-by-5-in [23-by-12-cm] metal loaf pan with nonstick cooking spray. Line the pan with an 8½-by-15-in [21.5-by-38-cm] strip of parchment paper so it covers the bottom of the pan and hangs over the long sides.

In a small bowl, sift together the flour, baking powder, and salt. Whisk in the finely chopped pecans. Set aside.

In a stand mixer fitted with the paddle attachment, beat the butter and cream cheese together with both of the sugars on medium speed until light and fluffy, about 3 to 4 minutes. Add the eggs, one at a time, beating well after each addition. Beat in the vanilla bean paste and bourbon.

Using a rubber or silicone spatula, fold half of the flour mixture into the batter by hand, just until combined and no streaks of white remain. Fold in the remaining dry ingredients. Scrape the batter into the prepared pan and spread evenly.

Bake for 50 to 60 minutes, or until a wooden skewer inserted into the center of the cake comes out clean or with only a few moist crumbs clinging to it.

Set the pan on a wire rack to let cool for 10 minutes. Then, grasping the overhanging parchment, lift the loaf out of the pan and set it on the cooling rack. Discard the parchment paper. Let cool completely before glazing.

TO MAKE THE GLAZE: In a large saucepan over medium heat, combine the brown sugar, butter, golden syrup, bourbon, and salt. Cook, stirring, until the butter melts and the sugar dissolves, about 2 minutes. Add the cream and bring to a boil. Cook, stirring occasionally, for exactly 1 minute. Remove from the heat and gently whisk in the confectioners' sugar and vanilla just until smooth. Let the glaze stand, stirring occasionally, until it cools to luke-warm but is still pourable.

Place the cake on a wire rack over a rimmed baking sheet. Pour half of the glaze over the top of the cake. Scatter the coarsely chopped pecans on top of the cake while the glaze is wet, mounding them slightly down the center of the cake. Drizzle the remaining glaze over the pecans. Let cool completely, allowing the glaze to set before slicing. Wrap the cake well in plastic wrap and store at room temperature for up to 3 days.

If a sticky bun and a layer cake fell in love and got married, this cake would be their baby. It's best served freshly baked and warm from the oven while the caramel and pecan topping is still gooey, but if made ahead of time, simply reheat in a low oven just until warm. Please note that the topping uses salted butter, while the cake calls for unsalted butter. This is important to get the perfect salty/sweet balance.

SALTED BUTTER PECAN CAKE

SERVES 8

TOPPING

½ cup [110 g] salted butter

1 cup [200 g] firmly packed golden brown sugar

3 Tbsp Golden Syrup (see page 17)

¼ tsp vanilla extract

1 Tbsp bourbon (optional)

1 cup [120 g] chopped pecans, toasted (see page 16)

1½ cups [150 g] sifted cake flour

1½ tsp baking powder

½ tsp fine sea salt

½ cup [110 g] unsalted butter, at room temperature

¾ cup [150 g] granulated sugar

¼ cup [50 g] firmly packed golden brown sugar

2 eggs

2 Tbsp Golden Syrup (see page 17)

⅔ cup [160 g] sour cream

1½ tsp vanilla extract

¼ tsp Maldon sea salt

Position a rack in the center of the oven. Preheat the oven to 350°F [180°C]. Coat a 9-in [23-cm] round cake pan with nonstick cooking spray. Set aside.

TO MAKE THE TOPPING: In a medium saucepan over medium-high heat, melt the salted butter. When the butter starts to bubble and turn golden, add the brown sugar and golden syrup. Decrease the heat to medium and stir until the sugar melts and starts to bubble. As soon as the mixture starts to boil, cook for 1 minute exactly, stirring continuously. Be very careful with this timing. (Boiling for more than a minute will result in caramel that will harden on the cake and be difficult to slice.) Remove from the heat and stir in the vanilla, bourbon, and pecans. Pour immediately into the prepared pan, using a small spatula to spread in an even layer. Set aside.

In a medium bowl, sift together the flour, baking powder, and fine sea salt. In a separate bowl, using an electric mixer set at medium speed, beat together the butter, granulated sugar, and brown sugar until light and fluffy, about 4 minutes. Beat in the eggs, one at a time, scraping down the sides of the bowl after each addition. Beat in the golden syrup, sour cream, and vanilla. With a rubber or silicone spatula, fold in the flour mixture by hand just until the batter is combined and no streaks of white remain. Spoon the batter into the pan with the topping, smoothing it evenly with a spatula.

Bake for 25 to 30 minutes, until a wooden skewer inserted into the center of the cake comes out clean.

Transfer the pan to a wire rack and let cool for 5 minutes. Invert the cake onto a serving plate. If any bits of caramel or nuts remain in the pan, simply scrape them from the pan and spread them over the cake with a spatula. Sprinkle the Maldon sea salt over the top of the cake. Serve the cake warm, cut into thick wedges.

Bacon love. Bacon is the crispy, chewy, temptress that makes everything from breakfast to a Bloody Mary to a BLT so enticing, and it gives this sweet-and-savory coffee cake irresistible appeal. You can candy the bacon while you prepare the cake batter, or, to save time, prepare it a few hours or up to 1 day in advance, along with the brown-sugar crumble. Both can be refrigerated separately in covered containers until you are ready to assemble the cake. Make sure to use thick-cut bacon, as it retains its crisp and chewy texture without drying out—or burning, when it is baked a second time as part of the crumble topping.

MAPLE SYRUP BREAKFAST CAKE
WITH CANDIED MAPLE-BACON CRUMBLE

SERVES 6 TO 8

CANDIED BACON

8 to 10 strips thick-cut bacon
¼ cup [50 g] firmly packed dark brown sugar

BROWN SUGAR CRUMBLE

¾ cup [105 g] all-purpose flour
¾ cup [150 g] firmly packed dark brown sugar
6 Tbsp [85 g] unsalted butter, melted
½ cup [60 g] coarsely chopped pecans, toasted (see page 16)

½ cup [120 ml] real maple syrup, preferably grade A ("dark with a robust taste"; see page 17)
1 cup [240 ml] buttermilk
½ cup [40 g] old-fashioned rolled oats
1½ cups [210 g] all-purpose flour
1 tsp baking powder
½ tsp baking soda
½ tsp fine sea salt
¾ cup [165 g] unsalted butter, at room temperature
1½ cups [300 g] granulated sugar
2 eggs
1 tsp vanilla extract
¼ tsp real maple flavoring

TO MAKE THE BACON: Preheat the oven to 400°F [200°C]. Line a rimmed baking sheet with aluminum foil.

Lay the bacon strips in a single layer on a wire rack and place on the prepared baking sheet.

Bake for 15 minutes without turning. Remove the baking sheet from the oven and sprinkle the partially cooked bacon evenly with the brown sugar. Return to the oven and continue baking for 6 to 8 minutes, until the bacon is cooked through and the brown sugar is bubbling. (The bacon will be cooked through but still chewy, rather than crisp, at this point. It will continue cooking as part of the crumble on top of the cake.) Let cool completely, chop coarsely, and set aside.

TO MAKE THE CRUMBLE: In a medium bowl, stir together the flour and brown sugar. Drizzle in the melted butter and stir with a fork until soft, moist crumbs form. Stir in the pecans and refrigerate until firm, about 30 minutes.

Position a rack in the center of the oven. Preheat the oven to 350°F [180°C]. Coat a 9-in [23-cm] round cake pan with nonstick cooking spray.

In a small saucepan over medium heat, simmer the maple syrup until it is reduced to ¼ cup [60 ml]. Decrease the heat to low, add the buttermilk and oats, and stir just until the buttermilk is warmed through, about 1 minute. Set aside to cool, about 30 minutes.

In a small bowl, sift together the flour, baking powder, baking soda, and salt. Set aside.

In the bowl of a stand mixer fitted with the paddle attachment, beat the butter with the sugar on medium speed until light and fluffy, 3 to 4 minutes. Add the eggs, one at a time, beating well after each addition. Beat in the vanilla and maple flavoring. Scrape down the sides of the bowl, add the cooled oatmeal-buttermilk mixture, and beat for a few seconds, just until incorporated. Using a rubber or silicone spatula, fold the dry ingredients into the batter in two additions, folding just until the batter is smooth and combined. Scrape the batter into the prepared pan, spreading evenly with the spatula.

Add the chopped candied bacon to the bowl with the crumble mixture and toss to mix. Sprinkle evenly over the surface of the batter.

Bake for 30 to 40 minutes, until a wooden skewer inserted into the center of the cake comes out clean.

Transfer the pan to a wire rack and let cool for 10 to 15 minutes. Serve warm, cut into wedges straight from the pan, or invert the cake onto a wire rack, and then invert again onto a cake platter or cake stand.

Although best served the day it is made, the cake can be stored in a covered cake carrier at room temperature for up to 2 days.

I adore Medjool dates. Considered the king of dates, they are rich and meaty and sweeter than honey—they're like candy that grows on trees. Warm and comforting and unapologetically sweet, sticky toffee pudding is an iconic British dessert that takes full advantage of all the lusciousness dates have to offer. As with all things warm and sweet, a scoop of vanilla ice cream is the perfect accompaniment.

STICKY TOFFEE PUDDING

SERVES 6 TO 8

12 oz [340 g] Medjool dates, pitted and coarsely chopped

1½ cups [360 ml] water

1¼ tsp baking soda

1½ cups [210 g] all-purpose flour

1 tsp baking powder

½ tsp fine sea salt

¾ cup [165 g] unsalted butter, at room temperature

¾ cup [150 g] firmly packed dark brown sugar

½ cup [100 g] granulated sugar

2 eggs

1 tsp vanilla extract

TOFFEE SAUCE

½ cup [110 g] unsalted butter

1½ cups [300 g] firmly packed dark brown sugar

1 cup [240 ml] heavy cream

¼ tsp Maldon sea salt

1 tsp vanilla extract

Position a rack in the center of the oven. Preheat the oven to 350°F [180°C]. Coat a 9-in [23-cm] round cake pan with nonstick cooking spray.

Combine the dates, water, and ¼ tsp of the baking soda in a deep saucepan. (Simmering the dates with a little baking soda helps to soften and break down the fibers in the dried fruit.) Bring to a gentle boil over medium-high heat. Decrease the heat to low and simmer the dates until they are tender and have absorbed much of the water, about 10 minutes. Remove from the heat and stir in the remaining 1 teaspoon baking soda. (The mixture will bubble when the baking soda is stirred in.)

While the dates are simmering, sift together the flour, baking powder, and salt into a medium bowl. Set aside.

In a separate bowl, with an electric hand mixer set at medium speed, beat the butter, brown sugar, and granulated sugar together until light and fluffy, 3 to 4 minutes. Add the eggs, one at a time, beating well after each addition. Beat the vanilla and the dates (along with any remaining soaking liquid) into the batter, just until combined. Using a rubber or silicone spatula, gently fold the dry ingredients into the batter by hand.

Scrape the batter into the prepared pan and smooth the top. Bake for 30 to 35 minutes, until a wooden skewer inserted into the center of the cake comes out clean.

TO MAKE THE SAUCE: Combine the butter and brown sugar in a saucepan over medium heat. Cook until the butter is melted and the sugar is dissolved. Add the cream and salt. Increase the heat to high and bring to a boil. Cook for 1 minute. Decrease the heat to medium-low and simmer until the sauce thickens, stirring occasionally, 5 to 7 minutes. Remove from the heat and stir in the vanilla.

When the cake is done, remove from the oven and poke the top all over with a fork. Spoon half of the warm sauce over the cake, spreading it over the surface and allowing it to saturate the cake completely. Place a large, deep-rimmed cake plate or platter over the pan and invert the cake. Remove the cake pan and pour the remaining warm sauce over the cake. Cut into wedges and serve warm.

This cake is best served the day it is made.

Pastel de tres leches, or "three-milks cake," is a beloved Latin American classic. Made from sponge cake drenched in a milky syrup made from sweetened condensed milk, evaporated milk, and heavy cream, it is served ice cold and traditionally topped with sweet meringue or whipped cream. Delicious when prepared in the classic method, *tres leches* is also open to a little creative interpretation. Top pieces of cake with sliced fresh peaches, mango, or raspberries, or stir fresh strawberry purée into the milky mixture before pouring it over the cake for a fresh spin on strawberry shortcake. In this version, I transform ordinary sweetened condensed milk into dulce de leche before stirring it together with cream, evaporated milk, and a splash of dark rum. Robust Mexican vanilla has a bold, spicy flavor that enhances the rich flavors in this classic cake.

PASTEL DE TRES LECHES

SERVES 12

CANDIED ALMONDS

1 egg white

½ cup [100 g] sugar

1 tsp ground cinnamon

1 cup [100 g] sliced almonds

HOT-MILK SPONGE CAKE

2 cups [240 g] sifted all-purpose flour

2 tsp baking powder

½ tsp fine sea salt

6 eggs, at room temperature

2 cups [400 g] sugar

1 teaspoon vanilla, preferably Mexican vanilla

¾ cup [180 ml] hot milk

DULCE DE TRES LECHES SYRUP

One 14-oz [400-g] can dulce de leche
  or DIY Dulce de Leche (page 91)

1 cup [240 ml] heavy cream

One 12-oz [360-ml] can evaporated milk

¼ tsp fine sea salt

¼ cup [60 ml] dark rum

1 tsp vanilla extract, preferably Mexican vanilla

WHIPPED CREAM TOPPING

2 cups [480 ml] heavy cream

¼ cup [50 g] sugar

1 tsp vanilla extract, preferably Mexican vanilla

TO MAKE THE CANDIED ALMONDS:
Position a rack in the center of the oven. Preheat the oven to 325°F [165°C]. Line a baking sheet with parchment paper.

In a medium bowl, beat the egg white with a hand mixer on high speed until frothy. Continue beating, adding the sugar and then the cinnamon in a steady stream. Beat just until thoroughly combined. Fold in the almonds by hand, using a rubber or silicone spatula.

Spread the almonds on the prepared baking sheet in as thin a layer as possible. Bake the almonds until they are crunchy and caramelized, about 30 minutes, stirring them every 5 minutes or so. Remove from the oven and let cool on the baking sheet until crisp. (The candied almonds can be stored in a covered container at room temperature for up to 1 week.)

Position a rack in the center of the oven. Preheat the oven to 350°F [180°C]. Spray a 9-by-13-in [23-by-33-cm] pan with nonstick cooking spray.

TO MAKE THE CAKE: In a medium bowl, sift together the flour, baking powder, and salt together three times to aerate.

In a stand mixer fitted with the whisk attachment, beat the eggs on high speed until thick, pale, and very fluffy, 3 to 4 minutes. With the mixer running, add the sugar, a little at a time, and beat until thick and frothy and thoroughly combined. Beat in the vanilla.

With a large balloon whisk, gently fold in the dry ingredients, about ½ cup [60 g] at a time, taking care not to deflate the batter. Fold in the hot milk and quickly scrape the batter into the prepared pan.

Bake for 30 to 35 minutes, until the cake is firm and golden and a wooden skewer inserted into the center of the cake comes out clean.

Transfer the pan to a wire rack and let cool completely. When cool, pierce the cake all over with a fork or skewer.

TO MAKE THE SYRUP: Combine the dulce de leche, cream, evaporated milk, and salt in a large saucepan over low heat and warm gently, whisking just until smooth. Remove from the heat and stir in the rum and vanilla.

Ladle the warm syrup over the cake, letting it seep in and gradually adding more as it is absorbed. Let the cake sit at room temperature until it is completely cool, then cover and refrigerate for at least 3 hours, and preferably overnight.

TO MAKE THE WHIPPED CREAM TOPPING: Right before serving, chill a large bowl and the beaters from an electric mixer in the refrigerator for 15 minutes until very cold. Combine the cream, sugar, and vanilla in the chilled bowl and beat until the cream forms softly mounding peaks.

Spread the whipped cream over the top of the cake and sprinkle with the candied almonds. Cut the cake into squares and serve cold.

The cake can be stored, covered in the refrigerator, for up to 2 days.

CROWD-PLEASER

If you are going to make just one caramel cake in your lifetime, it should be this one. The cake is tender and delicate, with a mild buttery flavor. It's the perfect sidekick to the real star of the show—three layers of rich caramel frosting. The classic method for making this frosting is a bit fussy, and the timing is crucial to get the distinctive and complex flavors we all crave. Unless you're strong enough to lift a cast-iron skillet with one hand while stirring a pot of boiling cream with the other, it's no easy feat. I've simplified things a little by adding a splash of cream to the initial caramel syrup to stop it from cooking any further or burning. This caramel "starter" can sit undisturbed while you turn your attention to the simmering cream and sugar—no need to rush, or worry about the caramel seizing, hardening, or burning if you don't move quickly enough.

CLASSIC SOUTHERN CARAMEL CAKE

SERVES 8 TO 10

3 cups [420 g] all-purpose flour

2 tsp baking powder

¼ tsp baking soda

1 tsp fine sea salt

1¼ cups [275 g] unsalted butter, at room temperature

2 cups [400 g] sugar

1 Tbsp vanilla extract

4 eggs, at room temperature

1⅓ cups [320 ml] buttermilk

CARAMEL FROSTING

3¾ cups [750 g] sugar

5 Tbsp [80 ml] water

2¼ cups [540 ml] heavy cream

¾ tsp fine sea salt

½ cup [110 g] unsalted butter

1 Tbsp vanilla extract

¾ tsp baking soda

Position a rack in the center of the oven. Preheat the oven to 350°F [180°C]. Coat three 8-in [20-cm] round cake pans with nonstick cooking spray and line the bottoms with parchment paper.

In a medium bowl, sift together the flour, baking powder, baking soda, and salt. Set aside.

In a stand mixer fitted with the paddle attachment, beat the butter at medium speed until light and creamy. Add the sugar and continue beating until the mixture is very pale and fluffy, 3 to 5 minutes. Scrape down the sides of the bowl and beat in the vanilla. Add the eggs, one at a time, beating well after each addition.

With the mixer on low, beat the dry ingredients into the batter in three additions, alternating with the buttermilk in two additions, beginning and ending with the dry ingredients. Beat for 10 to 15 seconds after each addition, just until the batter is smooth. Do not overbeat, or the final cake will be tough.

Divide the batter evenly between the prepared pans and spread the tops smooth with a spatula.

Bake for 25 to 28 minutes, until a wooden skewer inserted into the center of each cake comes out clean. Transfer the layers in their pans to wire racks, and let cool for 10 minutes. Invert the cakes onto the

Continued

racks, discarding the parchment paper, and let cool completely.

When completely cool and ready to frost, place one layer on a cardboard cake round, cake plate, or cake stand, bottom-side up and start the caramel frosting.

TO MAKE THE FROSTING: Combine 1¾ cups [350 g] of the sugar and 4 Tbsp [60 ml] of the water in a heavy-bottomed 3-qt [3-L] stainless-steel saucepan over medium heat. Cook, gently swirling the pan occasionally (do not stir), until the sugar dissolves and starts to caramelize. Increase the heat to high, bring to a boil, and cook until the syrup turns a deep golden amber (the color of an old penny), 4 to 6 minutes. The syrup should register 345° to 348°F [173° to 176°C] on an instant-read candy thermometer. Immediately remove the pan from the heat and pour in 1 cup [240 ml] of the cream. Using a long-handled wooden spoon (to avoid being splashed with hot caramel), stir in the cream until smooth. Set aside.

In a large 6-qt [6-L] pot, stir together the remaining 2 cups [400 g] sugar and 1¼ cups [300 ml] cream and the salt. Cook over medium heat, stirring occasionally, until the sugar dissolves, 3 to 4 minutes. Scrape the reserved caramel sauce into the pot and stir to combine. Raise the heat to medium-high and cook until the caramel mixture begins to boil and starts to thicken. Continue cooking, stirring occasionally, for 6 to 8 minutes, until the caramel registers 240°F [115°C] on a candy thermometer. (This is called the soft-ball stage: a spoonful of syrup dropped into ice water will not dissolve but instead will harden enough to form a pliable ball. See page 90.)

Remove the caramel from the heat and, using a wooden spoon, stir in the butter, vanilla, and baking soda. The baking soda will cause the caramel to foam and bubble wildly—keep stirring off the heat until the bubbling subsides. At this point the frosting will be very liquid and pourable, so allow it to cool, stirring, until it starts to contract and pull together slightly, and drops in heavy dollops from the spoon instead of a thin, steady, liquid stream. After a few minutes, the caramel will still be soft and warm, but firm enough to spread easily on the cake without dripping madly down the sides. Before you begin to assemble the cake, set aside 1 cup [220 g] of the caramel frosting to glaze the top.

TO FINISH THE CAKE: Spread a scant 1 cup [220 g] of the caramel frosting in a thin layer over the surface of the first cake layer, pushing it all the way to the edges. Top with the second cake layer and spread with another 1 cup [220 g] of frosting. Top with the final layer and quickly frost the top and then the sides of the cake with the remaining caramel. Allow the cake to rest for a few minutes, to give the frosting a chance to solidify a bit, 15 to 20 minutes.

To give the top of the cake a glossy finish, gently reheat the reserved 1 cup [220 g] caramel frosting just until warm and liquid, but not boiling hot. Pour this over the center of the cake, allowing it to cover the top of the cake and drip down the sides. Use an offset spatula to carefully smooth out the drips of caramel around the sides of the cake.

Store in a covered cake carrier at room temperature for up to 2 days.

At first glance this cake appears deceptively plain, but it is lush and rich. Delicate layers of vanilla bean cake are layered with German buttercream, a naughty combination of vanilla custard whipped together with a lavish amount of butter (see page 22). Permeated with the flavors of vanilla, burnt sugar, and cream, one bite will lure you into its downy embrace.

Make the caramelized sugar shards that decorate the top of this cake the day you want to serve it. If the weather is rainy or excessively humid, make the sugar shards as close to serving as possible. They will keep 3 to 4 hours on a dry day, and 1 to 2 hours if it is humid, before they start to get sticky.

CRÈME BRÛLÉE CAKE

SERVES 8 TO 10

3 cups [360 g] cake flour

3 tsp baking powder

1 tsp fine sea salt

¾ cup [180 ml] whole milk, at room temperature

¾ cup [180 g] sour cream, at room temperature

1 cup [220 g] unsalted butter, at room temperature

¼ cup [60 ml] canola or vegetable oil

2¼ cups [450 g] sugar

2 Tbsp vanilla bean paste

6 egg whites, at room temperature

BURNT SUGAR SYRUP

1 cup [200 g] sugar

1 cup [240 ml] warm water

MASCARPONE GERMAN BUTTERCREAM

3 cups [720 ml] whole milk

6 Tbsp [60 g] cornstarch

3 eggs

3 egg yolks

3 cups [600 g] sugar

¼ tsp fine sea salt

3 cups [660 g] unsalted butter, at room temperature

½ cup [120 g] mascarpone cheese, at room temperature

2 Tbsp vanilla bean paste

CARAMELIZED SUGAR SHARDS

1 cup [200 g] sugar

Position a rack in the center of the oven. Preheat the oven to 350°F [180°C]. Coat three 8-in [20-cm] or 9-in [23-cm] round cake pans with nonstick cooking spray. Line the bottoms with parchment paper.

Sift together the cake flour, baking powder, and salt into a medium bowl. In a separate medium bowl, whisk together the milk and sour cream.

In a stand mixer fitted with the paddle attachment, beat the butter and oil together on medium speed until creamy. Increase the speed to medium-high, add the sugar, and beat until light and fluffy, 3 to 5 minutes. Beat in the vanilla paste and vanilla extract. Stop the mixer and scrape down the sides of the bowl. With the mixer on medium-high speed, beat in half of the egg whites, just until combined. Stop the mixer and scrape down the sides of the bowl again. Beat in the remaining egg whites just until smooth.

With the mixer on low, beat the dry ingredients into the batter in three additions, alternating with two additions of the sour cream mixture and beginning and ending with the dry ingredients. Beat for 10 to 15 seconds after each addition, just until the batter is smooth. Do not overbeat, or the final cake will be tough. Divide the batter evenly between the prepared cake pans, using a spatula to smooth the tops. Bake for 25 to 30 minutes for 8-in [20-cm] layers or 22 to 28 minutes for 9-in [23-cm] layers, until a wooden skewer inserted into the center of each cake comes out clean.

TO MAKE THE BURNT SUGAR SYRUP:

While the cake layers are baking, combine the sugar and ¼ cup [60 ml] of the warm water in a 2-qt [2-L] stainless-steel saucepan over medium heat. Cook, gently swirling the pan occasionally, without stirring, until the sugar dissolves and starts to caramelize. Increase the heat to high and

Continued

boil until it turns a golden amber color, 4 to 6 minutes. Immediately remove the pan from the heat and pour in the remaining ¾ cup [180 ml] warm water. Stir, using a long-handled wooden spoon to avoid being splashed with hot caramel, until the caramel dissolves.

(The Burnt Sugar Syrup can be used immediately, or, if making it in advance, refrigerate in a covered container for up to 1 month. Just make sure to warm it up before brushing it on your cake layers.)

When the cake layers are done, transfer the pans to wire racks and let cool for 10 minutes. Invert the layers onto the racks, remove the pans, and peel off the parchment paper. While the cake layers are still warm, brush the bottoms and sides of each layer with the warm Burnt Sugar Syrup, making sure to use all the syrup. Let the cake layers cool completely before filling and frosting.

TO MAKE THE BUTTERCREAM: In a medium heatproof bowl, whisk together ½ cup [120 ml] of the milk with the cornstarch to dissolve. Whisk in the eggs and egg yolks. Set aside.

In a 3-qt [3-L] stainless-steel saucepan, stir together the remaining 2½ cups [600 ml] milk and the sugar. Stir over medium heat until the sugar is dissolved. Increase the heat to medium-high and bring to a boil. Remove from the heat and briskly whisk ½ cup [120 ml] of the hot milk mixture into the egg mixture to temper it. Whisk in an additional ½ cup [120 ml] hot milk. When the mixture is smooth, whisk in the remaining milk and the salt. Return the mixture to the saucepan.

Over medium-high heat, whisk the custard continuously until it thickens and comes to a low boil, with large bubbles that rise to the surface, plopping slowly. Continue whisking, without stopping, for 1 to 2 minutes. This will thicken the custard and cook the eggs completely. Do not cook any longer than 2 minutes, as the cornstarch will actually start to lose its thickening ability and the custard will become thin and soupy as it cools.

Pour the warm custard through a fine-mesh sieve into a large bowl. Cover with plastic wrap, pressing it onto the surface of the custard to prevent a skin from forming. Refrigerate until very cold, at least 3 hours and preferably overnight.

When cold and firm, scrape the custard into the bowl of a stand mixer fitted with the whisk attachment. Beat the custard on low for a few seconds to loosen it. Increase the mixer speed to medium and beat in the softened butter, 2 Tbsp at a time. Continue beating, adding the butter a little at a time, until it is fully incorporated and the buttercream is fluffy and thick enough to spread. Beat in the softened mascarpone and vanilla bean paste, just until combined.

TO FINISH THE CAKE: Place the first syrup-soaked cake layer on a cardboard cake round or cake stand, bottom-side up. Top with one-fourth of the buttercream, spreading it over the surface of the cake in an even layer all the way to the edges. Top with the second cake layer and spread with the same amount of buttercream. Top with the third cake layer. Frost the top and sides of the cake with a thin coat of buttercream to form a crumb coat (see page 21). Refrigerate for 30 minutes to set.

Spread the top and sides of the cake generously with the remaining buttercream, smoothing it evenly with an offset spatula. Refrigerate the cake in a covered cake carrier for up to 24 hours before serving. Let the cake come to room temperature 1 to 2 hours before slicing. Up to 1 hour before serving, decorate the top of the cake with broken, caramelized sugar shards. Store at room temperature for up to 2 days (sugar shards may soften and start to melt after a few hours, but are still tasty).

TO MAKE THE CARAMELIZED SUGAR SHARDS: Sprinkle the sugar in an even layer in a large, heavy-bottomed stainless-steel saucepan. Heat over medium-high heat until it begins to melt around the edges. Stir with a fork (the sugar may clump or form lumps, but will smooth out as it melts). When the sugar has melted into a syrup, bring to a boil and cook until it turns a golden amber caramel color (about 340°F [170°C] degrees on an instant-read candy thermometer). Immediately pour the syrup onto a rimmed baking sheet, tipping the pan so the syrup coats about half of the pan in a thin, even layer. Let cool completely, about 15 minutes. (I choose not to grease the pan, as the oil tends to leave a slick film on the sugar shards.)

To dislodge the hardened sugar, tap gently with a small mallet or the back of a heavy knife to break it into large pieces. Once broken, you can dislodge the caramel shards with your fingers or the tip of an offset spatula. To make smaller pieces, place the large shards in a self-sealing plastic bag and give them a few firm whacks with the mallet or knife. Use the shards and any caramel dust to decorate the top of the cake.

CITRUS

Imagine a world without lemons. No lemon meringue pie, or proper British lemon curd. No lemonade or lemon drops or lemon bars. No lovely loaf of lemon cake, cut into thick slices and served with a hot cup of tea, perfumed and glazed with the zest and juice from the world's sunniest fruit. Now imagine your kitchen without limes and oranges, or ruby red grapefruit, or tangerines. It's too terrible to contemplate.

Cakes infused with citrus have a bright intensity that I love. With their bold colors and refreshing tart-and-tangy flavors, lemons and limes, oranges, clementines, and grapefruits give even the simplest of cakes a quality the English would christen "moreish," meaning one bite will never be quite enough.

CITRUS BASICS

The nice thing about citrus fruit is that there are so many different ingredients in one little package, from the colorful zest grated from the rind of the fruit—packed with essential oils and intense flavor—to the juicy flesh and tangy juices inside. Following are tips on how to extract as much flavor and fun from the produce department's zestiest fruits.

CITRUS SUPREMACY

Citrus segments are often referred to as "supremes." Here is how to peel and segment fruits like oranges, lemons, limes, and grapefruits.

Using a sharp knife, cut a thin slice from the top (stem end) and bottom (blossom end) of the fruit. Set the fruit on a cutting board, bottom-side down. (This will keep the fruit steady as you peel it.)

Using the knife, cut off the rind (this includes both the colorful skin and the layer of bitter white pith beneath) lengthwise in strips, following the curve of the fruit from top to bottom.

Hold the completely peeled fruit in your nondominant hand over a bowl to collect the juices. Each citrus segment is encased on either side by a strong membrane. Slide the blade of a sharp paring knife between the membranes to loosen a fruit segment. Let the segment drop into the bowl and proceed with the next. When all the segments have been released into the bowl, squeeze the empty membranes to release any remaining juices into the bowl.

KEEP IT ZESTY

Zest is an appropriate name for the brightly colored outer rind of citrus fruit, for that is where all the aromatic essential oils and most of the intense flavors reside. Just a teaspoon or two of lemon, lime, orange—even grapefruit—zest enlivens the flavor and aroma of any cake batter or buttercream you prepare.

One way to maximize the zingy citrus flavor in your recipe is to turn your plain granulated sugar into citrus sugar. Using a Microplane zester, grate the citrus fruit directly over a small bowl containing the sugar in the recipe. (Be sure to remove only the colorful part of the skin, not the bitter white pith underneath.) To extract every drop of flavor possible, rub the sugar and zest together with your fingertips. When massaged together, the sharp sugar crystals help release all the essential oils in the citrus zest; the sugar will become damp and sandy and deeply fragrant.

If you don't have a Microplane zester, you can use a swivel vegetable peeler to remove the thin layer of zest and combine it with the sugar in a food processor. A few short pulses will pulverize the zest, releasing the citrus flavor into the sugar.

Lemon zest, lemon juice, and lemon oil combine to give this simple cake real zing. You might be tempted to skip the lemon oil, but I hope you won't. It adds a wonderful fragrance and intense lemon flavor that lemon extract just can't match. Cold-pressed from the zest of oranges, limes, or lemons, citrus oils are concentrated and fragile. They must be refrigerated once the bottle is open, but even then, they don't last forever.

CROWD-PLEASER

LUSCIOUS LEMON LOAF

SERVES 6 TO 8

Position a rack in the center of the oven. Preheat the oven to 325°F [165°C]. Coat a 9-by-5-in [23-by-12-cm] metal loaf pan with nonstick cooking spray. Line the pan with an 8½-by-15-in [21.5-by-38-cm] strip of parchment paper so it covers the bottom of the pan and hangs over the long sides.

Put the sugar in a small bowl. Using a Microplane zester, grate the zest from the lemons onto the sugar. Rub the zest into the sugar with your fingertips until the sugar is sandy and moist and fragrant with lemon. Set aside.

Cut the lemons in half. Using a citrus reamer, squeeze the juice from the lemons into another small bowl.

In a third small bowl, whisk together ¼ cup [60 ml] of the fresh lemon juice (you should have about 2 Tbsp remaining; set aside to use for the icing), the sour cream, vanilla, and lemon oil. Set the reserved lemon juice and the sour-cream mixture aside.

In a medium bowl, sift together the flour, baking powder, baking soda, and salt. Set aside.

In a stand mixer fitted with the paddle attachment, beat the butter and oil together at medium speed just until creamy. Add the lemon sugar and beat until light and fluffy, 3 to 4 minutes. Add the eggs, one at a time, beating well after each addition and scraping down the bowl as you go. Decrease the mixer speed to low and beat in the sour-cream mixture. Add the dry ingredients in two additions, beating on low for a few seconds after each.

Scrape the batter into the prepared pan and smooth the top with a spatula. Bake for 55 to 65 minutes. Do not check the cake until it has been in the oven for at least 40 minutes, as it might sink in the middle. The cake is done when a wooden skewer inserted into the center of the cake comes out clean.

1½ cups [300 g] granulated sugar

2 large lemons

½ cup [120 g] sour cream

1 tsp vanilla extract

1¼ tsp lemon oil

1½ cups [245 g] all-purpose flour

1½ tsp baking powder

½ tsp fine sea salt

½ cup [110 g] unsalted butter, at room temperature

¼ cup [60 ml] canola oil

3 eggs, at room temperature

LEMON ICING

2 Tbsp unsalted butter, at room temperature

2 Tbsp freshly squeezed lemon juice (from above)

⅛ teaspoon lemon oil

1½ to 2 cups [180 g to 240 g] confectioners' sugar, sifted

Continued

Transfer the loaf, still in the pan, to a wire rack and let cool for 10 minutes. Grasping the overhanging parchment, lift the loaf out of the pan and set it on the rack. Let cool completely before icing. Discard the parchment paper.

TO MAKE THE ICING: In a medium bowl, whisk together the butter, the reserved 2 Tbsp lemon juice, and the lemon oil. Sift in 1½ cups [180 g] confectioners' sugar and whisk until smooth and creamy. If a stiffer icing is desired, whisk in up to ½ cup [60 g] more confectioners' sugar.

When the cake is completely cool, spread or drizzle the top of the cake with the Lemon Icing.

Cut into thick slices to serve. Store wrapped well in plastic wrap or in a tightly covered container at room temperature for up to 2 days.

1 cup [140 g] all-purpose flour

½ cup [65 g] almond meal (made with finely ground natural almonds)

½ cup [65 g] stone-ground yellow cornmeal

2 tsp baking powder

1 tsp fine sea salt

1 cup [220 g] unsalted butter, at room temperature

1½ cups [300 g] granulated sugar

3 eggs, at room temperature

½ cup [120 g] whole-milk yogurt

Grated zest and juice from 2 limes (about 4 Tbsp juice)

¼ tsp almond extract

LIME SYRUP

½ cup [120 ml] fresh lime juice

½ cup [100 g] granulated sugar

LIME ICING

2 to 3 Tbsp freshly squeezed lime juice

Grated zest of 1 lime

1 cup [120 g] confectioners' sugar, sifted

Almonds and stone-ground cornmeal dance merrily together in this rustic cake, its wonderful nubby texture brightened with a sharp squeeze of lime. Although it can be enjoyed any time of year, its simplicity seems particularly suited to lazy summer days. When blackberries are in season, I like to stir a few handfuls of berries together with some of the lime syrup, crushing a few to release their juices, to spoon over chunky slices of cake. You'll need a nice deep cake pan to accommodate the generous batter. If your pan is too shallow, the batter will overflow, or it will start to rise—and with nothing to cling to, will collapse onto itself and sink deeply in the center. One lime yields approximately 2 tablespoons of juice, so for this cake you will need about 7 limes.

CORNMEAL-LIME CAKE

SERVES 8

Position a rack in the center of the oven. Preheat the oven to 350°F [180°C]. Coat a 9-in [23-cm] round cake pan or a springform pan with 3-in [7.5-cm] sides with nonstick cooking spray. Line the pan with parchment paper.

In a medium bowl, whisk together the flour, almond meal, cornmeal, baking powder, and salt. Set aside.

In the bowl of a stand mixer fitted with the paddle attachment, beat the butter and sugar together on medium-high speed until light and creamy, 3 to 5 minutes. Beat in the eggs, one at a time, beating well after each addition. Scrape down the sides of the bowl as needed. Beat in the yogurt, lime juice and zest, and almond extract.

With the mixer on low, beat in the dry ingredients just until combined, 15 to 20 seconds. Scrape the batter into the prepared pan and bake for 45 to 55 minutes, until a wooden skewer inserted into the center of the cake comes out clean.

TO MAKE THE LIME SYRUP: While the cake is baking, stir together the lime juice and sugar in a medium saucepan over medium-high heat just until the sugar dissolves. Increase the heat to high and boil for 30 seconds. Remove from the heat and cover to keep warm.

Transfer the cake to a wire rack and let cool in the pan for 10 minutes. Unmold, and discard the parchment paper. Transfer the cake to a serving plate or cake stand. While the cake is still warm, brush the warm lime syrup over the top and around the sides of the cake, adding more syrup as it soaks in. Let the cake cool completely before icing.

TO MAKE THE LIME ICING: In a small bowl, whisk together 2 Tbsp of the lime juice, the lime zest, and the sifted confectioners' sugar until smooth. If too thick, add more lime juice, 1 tsp at a time, until the right consistency is achieved.

Pour the icing in a thin, even layer over the top of the cake, leaving the sides bare. Store the cake well wrapped in plastic wrap or tightly covered in a cake carrier or other container, at room temperature for up to 3 days.

My husband spent his formative years battling cold winters throughout the Midwest, and so, after settling in Southern California, he swears the only way he'll ever watch the seasons change again is on The Weather Channel. Mild winters mean that when the rest of the country is shoveling snow, we're harvesting bumper crops of golden Meyer lemons. Even a notoriously bad gardener like myself can manage to coax a handful of lemons from my little potted backyard tree. A cross between a lemon and a mandarin orange, Meyer lemons are mildly acidic, with a mellow sweetness and an intoxicating floral aroma. They make the most delicious fresh lemonade—and lemon cake. Combined with the tiny but powerful kumquat, one bite of this cake is like a taste of California sunshine.

CALIFORNIA SUNSHINE CAKE

SERVES 8

1¾ cups [245 g] all-purpose flour

1 tsp baking powder

¾ tsp fine sea salt

1⅔ cups [330 g] sugar, plus 1 Tbsp

2 medium Meyer lemons

5 oz [140 g] kumquats (about 10)

¾ cup [165 g] unsalted butter, at room temperature

½ cup [120 g] cream cheese, at room temperature

4 eggs, at room temperature

1 tsp vanilla extract

MEYER LEMON GLAZE

1½ cups [180 g] confectioners' sugar

2 to 3 Tbsp freshly squeezed Meyer lemon juice (from above), plus more if needed

Position a rack in the center of the oven. Preheat the oven to 300°F [150°C]. Coat a 9-in [23-cm] round cake pan or a spring-form pan with nonstick cooking spray and line the bottom with parchment paper.

Sift together the flour, baking powder, and salt into a medium bowl, Set aside.

Put the 1⅔ cups [330 g] sugar in a small bowl. Using a Microplane zester, grate the zest from the Meyer lemons onto the sugar. Rub the zest into the sugar with your fingertips until the sugar is sandy and moist and fragrant with lemon. Set aside.

Cut the lemons in half. Using a citrus reamer, squeeze the juice from the lemons into another small bowl. (You should have about 6 Tbsp of juice, enough for the cake and the glaze.) Set aside.

On a cutting board, slice each kumquat in half, removing any seeds with the tip of a paring knife. Combine the seeded kumquats and 4 Tbsp [60 ml] of the reserved lemon juice in a blender or food processor and purée into a thick, smooth paste (you should have about ½ cup [120 ml]). Set aside.

In a stand mixer fitted with the paddle attachment, beat the butter and cream cheese together on low speed until creamy. Add the lemon sugar, increase the mixer speed to medium-high, and beat until light and fluffy, 3 to 4 minutes. Scrape down the sides of the bowl. Add the eggs, one at a time, beating well after each addition. Beat in the vanilla and the kumquat purée. The batter may appear a little curdled at this point, but will smooth out when the dry ingredients are added.

With a rubber or silicone spatula, fold the dry ingredients into the batter by hand in two additions, just until the batter is smooth and combined.

Scrape the batter into the prepared pan and smooth the top with a spatula. Sprinkle evenly with the 1 Tbsp sugar. Bake for 45 to 55 minutes, until a wooden skewer inserted into the center of the cake comes out clean. Transfer the cake to a wire rack and let cool in the pan for 10 minutes. Invert the cake onto the rack and discard the parchment paper. Invert the cake again onto a cake plate so the top of the cake is right side up.

TO MAKE THE GLAZE: Sift the confectioners' sugar into a small bowl and whisk in the 2 Tbsp reserved lemon juice until smooth. If the glaze is too thick, whisk in additional lemon juice or water as needed, 1 tsp at a time.

Spread or drizzle the glaze over the top of the cake, allowing the excess to drip down the sides. Store the cake well wrapped in plastic wrap or in a covered cake carrier at room temperature for up to 3 days.

Bill Yosses, former White House pastry chef, developed an inventive technique for infusing his lemon cake with more flavor and moisture: He blends fresh lemon segments into the batter. As the cake bakes, the fruit dissolves, leaving behind tart little pockets of flavor. I've employed the same technique here in a simple ricotta pound cake, lacing the batter with crimson morsels of sweet-tart blood oranges. I like to serve slices of this pound cake with a stunning blood orange compote inspired by my friend, fellow food writer and cookbook author Susan Russo. Gorgeous slices of tart blood oranges are bathed in a warm honey syrup infused with vanilla bean, star anise, and whole cloves. The compote can be served chilled or at room temperature.

BLOOD ORANGE COMPOTE

1 cup [240 ml] water

¼ cup [60 ml] blood orange juice

½ cup [170 ml] mild honey

½ cup [100 g] granulated sugar

2 tablespoons pomegranate molasses

½ vanilla bean, split lengthwise

3 whole star anise

4 whole cloves

8 medium blood oranges, peeled and sliced crosswise into rounds

3 cups [420 g] all-purpose flour

1 tsp baking powder

1 tsp fine sea salt

2¾ cups [550 g] granulated sugar

3 medium blood oranges

2 Tbsp pomegranate molasses

¼ tsp orange oil

1 tsp vanilla extract

1½ cups [330 g] unsalted butter, at room temperature

2 cups [480 g] whole-milk ricotta cheese, at room temperature

6 eggs, at room temperature

Confectioners' sugar for dusting (optional)

BLOOD ORANGE-RICOTTA POUND CAKE WITH SPICED BLOOD ORANGE COMPOTE

SERVES 12

TO MAKE THE BLOOD ORANGE COMPOTE: In a medium saucepan over medium-high heat, combine the water, orange juice, honey, sugar, and pomegranate molasses and bring to a boil. Decrease the heat to low and add the vanilla bean, star anise, and cloves. Simmer, partially covered, for 10 to 15 minutes, until syrupy. Add the oranges and simmer gently for just 5 minutes more (any longer and the oranges will become too soft, and start to fall apart). Remove the pan from the heat and spoon the compote and poaching syrup into a bowl. Set aside and let cool. Remove the star anise and cloves.

Position a rack in the center of the oven. Preheat the oven to 325°F [165°C]. Coat a 10-cup [2.4-L] Bundt pan with nonstick cooking spray.

Sift the flour, baking powder, and salt together into a medium bowl. Set aside.

Using a Microplane zester, grate the zest from the oranges onto the sugar. Rub the zest into the sugar with your fingertips

Continued

until the sugar is sandy and moist and fragrant with orange. Set aside.

Remove any remaining peel and the pith from the oranges (see page 110). When completely peeled, hold the oranges, one at a time, over a small bowl; cut the orange segments away from their protective membranes, allowing the segments to drop into the bowl. Squeeze any remaining juice from the empty membranes into the bowl and discard the membrane. Using your fingers, tear each citrus segment into thirds. Stir in the pomegranate molasses, orange oil, and vanilla. Set aside.

In a stand mixer fitted with the paddle attachment, beat the butter and orange sugar together on medium-high speed until light and creamy, 3 to 4 minutes. Add the ricotta and beat just until combined. Scrape down the sides of the bowl. Add the eggs, one at a time, beating well after each addition. Decrease the mixer speed to low and add blood orange-pomegranate mixture to the batter, beating just until combined, 15 to 20 seconds.

Add the dry ingredients to the batter, one-third at a time, and beat for about 10 to 15 seconds after each addition. Scrape the batter into the prepared pan and bake for 60 to 70 minutes, until a wooden skewer inserted into the center of the cake comes out clean. Transfer the cake to a wire rack and let cool in the pan for 10 to 15 minutes. Invert the cake onto the wire rack. Brush the cake with a little of the poaching syrup from the compote for extra flavor, if you like, or just sprinkle with cake with confectioners' sugar.

The blood oranges are delicious served warm, at room temperature, or chilled. If not serving immediately, cover the compote and refrigerate for up to 2 days.

Store the cake in a covered cake carrier at room temperature for up to 2 days.

The illustrious Brown Derby restaurant in Los Angeles, whimsically shaped like a man's hat, catered to the Hollywood elite; there gossip columnist Louella Parsons famously battled with her rival Hedda Hopper to win the best table at lunch. Legend has it that the famous Brown Derby Grapefruit Cake was created for the dieting Parsons, who demanded a healthier option for dessert. It was an instant hit, even if it wasn't the figure-friendly dessert Parsons had hoped for. The original Brown Derby closed, but you can still taste a version of this cake at Valerie's Confections in Los Angeles. In my version, I've added a little extra zing with a rosy grapefruit jelly slicked between the layers and glossed over the top of the frosted cake. Don't be tempted to use bottled grapefruit juice cocktail—it's too sweet. Many produce departments stock freshly squeezed orange and grapefruit juices for your convenience, if you don't want to squeeze your own.

RUBY RED GRAPEFRUIT CAKE

SERVES 8 TO 10

RUBY RED GRAPEFRUIT JELLY

3 Tbsp low-or-no-sugar-needed powdered pectin

1½ cups [300 g] granulated sugar

2½ cups [600 ml] freshly squeezed Ruby Red grapefruit juice (from about 5 grapefruit)

½ cup [120 ml] freshly squeezed tangerine juice

¼ cup [60 ml] freshly squeezed lemon juice

2 Tbsp grenadine (optional)

RUBY RED CAKE

3 Ruby Red grapefruits

1¾ cups [175 g] sifted cake flour

1½ tsp baking powder

½ tsp fine sea salt

1¼ cups [250 g] sugar

½ cup [120 ml] canola or vegetable oil

½ cup [120 ml] orange juice or milk

6 egg yolks

1 tsp grated lemon zest

1 tsp vanilla extract

¼ tsp orange extract

¼ tsp lemon extract

6 egg whites

¼ tsp cream of tartar

CREAM-CHEESE FROSTING

½ cup [110 g] unsalted butter, at room temperature

12 ounces [340 g] cream cheese, at room temperature

2 Tbsp Ruby Red Grapefruit Jelly (from above)

4 to 5 cups [480 to 500 g] confectioners' sugar, sifted

TO MAKE THE JELLY: In a medium bowl, whisk together the pectin and sugar. Set aside. In a 3-qt [3-L] saucepan over medium-low heat, stir together the grapefruit, tangerine, and lemon juices. Whisk in the pectin mixture, stirring until dissolved. Bring to a rolling boil over high heat and cook, stirring constantly, until the jelly is thick and syrupy but still pourable, 3 to 5 minutes. Remove from the heat and stir in the grenadine to enhance the pink color of the jelly, if you like. Strain the jelly into two 1-pt [480-ml] jars. Let cool, cover, and refrigerate for up to 1 week.

TO MAKE THE CAKE: Position a rack in the center of the oven. Preheat the oven to 350°F [180°C]. Coat the bottoms *only* of two 9-in [23-cm] round cake pans with nonstick cooking spray. Line the bottoms with parchment paper.

Using a Microplane zester, grate the zest from 1 grapefruit. Cut the grapefruit in half and use a citrus reamer to squeeze the juice into a small bowl. Set aside the zest and juice. Remove the peel and pith from the 2 remaining grapefruits and then slice them into ½ inch [12 mm] thick rounds (see page 110). Store the grapefruit segments in a covered bowl until you are ready to assemble the cake.

Continued

121

In a large bowl, sift together the cake flour, baking powder, and salt. Whisk in 1 cup [200 g] of the sugar.

In a second large bowl, whisk together the oil, orange juice, egg yolks, ¼ cup [60 ml] of the reserved grapefruit juice, and the grapefruit zest, the lemon zest, and the vanilla, orange, and lemon extracts. Whisk the egg-yolk mixture into the dry ingredients until smooth.

In the clean, grease-free bowl of a stand mixer fitted with the whisk attachment, beat the egg whites and cream of tartar together on low speed until opaque and frothy, about 1 minute. Increase the speed to medium-high and beat until soft peaks form, 2 to 3 minutes. Continue beating, adding the remaining ¼ cup [50 g] sugar, 1 Tbsp at a time, until the egg whites are firm and glossy, about 1 minute more.

With a rubber or silicone spatula, fold one-third of the whites into the cake batter to lighten it. Gently fold the remaining whipped egg whites into the batter just until incorporated, taking care not to deflate them.

Divide the batter evenly between the prepared pans, spreading the batter tops smooth with a spatula. Bake until the layers are golden and spring back when pressed gently in the center, and when a wooden skewer inserted into the center of each cake comes out clean, 20 to 25 minutes.

Cool the layers, upside-down in their pans, on a wire rack for 30 minutes. Run a thin, offset spatula around the edges of the pans to loosen the cakes. Invert onto the racks and discard the parchment paper. Let the layers cool completely.

TO MAKE THE FROSTING: In a stand mixer fitted with the paddle attachment, beat together the butter, cream cheese, and grapefruit jelly until creamy. Add 4 cups [480 g] of the sifted confectioners' sugar and beat until smooth and spreadable, 2 to 3 minutes. If the frosting seems too thin, add as much of the remaining confectioners' sugar as needed to reach the desired consistency.

TO FINISH THE CAKE: Place one layer on a cardboard cake round, cake plate, or cake stand, bottom-side up. Spread with one-fourth of the cream cheese frosting. Melt ¾ cup [225 g] of the grapefruit jelly in a small saucepan over medium-low heat. Spoon the melted jelly over the frosting and spread in an even layer with an offset spatula. Give the jelly a few seconds to set. Drain the reserved grapefruit slices, reserving a few of the prettiest ones to garnish the top of the cake, and break the remaining segments into two or three pieces. Scatter the pieces of grapefruit over the jelly. Top with the second cake layer. Frost the top and sides of the cake generously with the remaining cream cheese frosting, spreading it smoothly with an offset spatula. Refrigerate the cake until the frosting is cold and very firm.

Melt 1 cup [300 g] of the grapefruit jelly and pour it over the top of the cake, spreading the jelly into a thin, even layer and allowing the excess to drip down the sides of the cake. Arrange the reserved grapefruit slices decoratively on top of the cake. Store the cake in a tightly covered cake carrier or other container and refrigerate until ready to serve.

Although this cake is best eaten the day it is assembled, the jelly, the grapefruit slices, and the cream cheese frosting can all be made up to 3 days in advance and refrigerated until needed.

2½ cups [500 g] granulated sugar

3 Tbsp grated lemon zest

1½ cups [210 g] all-purpose flour

1½ cups [180 g] cake flour

3 tsp baking powder

¼ tsp baking soda

1¼ tsp fine sea salt

1 cup [240 g] sour cream, at room temperature

¼ cup [60 ml] freshly squeezed lemon juice

½ cup [110 g] unsalted butter, at room temperature

½ cup [120 ml] canola or vegetable oil

3 eggs, at room temperature

2 egg yolks, at room temperature

1 tsp vanilla extract

1 cup [120 g] very finely chopped walnuts

WHITE-CHOCOLATE CREAM-CHEESE FROSTING

12 oz [340 g] white chocolate, coarsely chopped

1 lb [455 g] cream cheese, at room temperature

½ cup [110 g] unsalted butter, at room temperature

¼ tsp lemon oil or ½ tsp lemon extract

2 Tbsp freshly squeezed lemon juice

1 cup [120 g] confectioners' sugar, plus more if needed

CANDIED WALNUTS

6 Tbsp [75 g] granulated sugar

3 Tbsp water

2 cups [240 g] chopped walnuts

The Ivy, a restaurant in West Hollywood famous for its cozy setting, big portions, and celebrity couples looking for attention, is also famous for a made-to-order lemon cake studded with walnuts and layered with a white-chocolate lemon mousse and whipped cream. My streamlined version features a tall cylinder of lemony sour-cream cake swathed in white-chocolate cream-cheese frosting and encrusted all over with candied walnuts. Definitely starlet-worthy.

WHITE CHOCOLATE-LEMON WALNUT CAKE

SERVES 8 TO 10

Position a rack in the center of the oven. Preheat the oven to 350°F [180°C]. Coat three 8-in [20-cm] or 9-in [23-cm] round cake pans with nonstick cooking spray. Line the bottoms with parchment paper.

Place the sugar in a small bowl, add the lemon zest, and rub the sugar and lemon zest together until the sugar is moist and sandy and fragrant with lemon. Set aside.

In a medium bowl, sift together the all-purpose flour, cake flour, baking powder, baking soda, and salt. Set aside.

Stir the sour cream and lemon juice together in a small bowl. Set aside.

In a stand mixer fitted with the paddle attachment, beat the butter and oil together on low speed until creamy and emulsified, 1 to 2 minutes. Add the lemon sugar and beat on medium speed until light and fluffy, 4 to 5 minutes. Scrape down the sides of the bowl and add the eggs and egg yolks, one at a time, beating well after each addition. Beat in the vanilla.

On low speed, beat the dry ingredients into the batter in three additions, beating after each addition just until combined, 10 to 15 seconds. Alternate with 2 additions of the sour-cream mixture, beginning and ending with the dry ingredients. With a rubber or silicone spatula, fold in the finely chopped walnuts.

Divide the batter evenly between the prepared pans and smooth the tops with a spatula. Bake for 25 to 30 minutes, until a wooden skewer inserted into the center of each cake comes out clean.

Transfer the cakes to wire racks and let cool in the pans for 10 minutes. Invert onto the racks and discard the parchment paper. Let cool completely.

TO MAKE THE FROSTING: Spread the chopped white chocolate in a single layer on a microwave-safe plate. Microwave on high for 15 seconds. The chocolate should be soft and shiny, but still holding its shape. Stir until smooth. If the chocolate is not completely melted, heat in 15-second increments, stirring until smooth. Set aside.

In a stand mixer fitted with the paddle attachment, beat the cream cheese on high speed until smooth. Scrape down the bowl. With the mixer on low, beat in the melted white chocolate. Beat in the butter and lemon oil until thick and creamy. Beat in the lemon juice and then the confectioners' sugar. The frosting should be thick and spreadable. If too thin, beat in a little more confectioners' sugar until it reaches the right consistency. Set aside.

TO MAKE THE CANDIED WALNUTS: Combine the sugar and water in a medium saucepan. Place over medium heat and cook, swirling the pan occasionally, until the sugar dissolves. Add the chopped walnuts and bring the mixture to a boil, stirring the walnuts to coat with the sugar syrup. Decrease the heat to medium and cook for 2 to 3 minutes, stirring occasionally, until the syrup coating the nuts is thick and sticky. Scrape the nut mixture onto a baking sheet, using a fork to separate them if necessary, and let cool in a single layer. When cool, the nuts should be crisp. Chop the candied nuts very finely with a sharp knife, or in a food processor fitted with the metal blade with short pulses, until very finely ground.

TO FINISH THE CAKE: Place one cake layer on a round cardboard cake round, cake plate, or cake stand. Spread evenly with one-fourth of the frosting. Top with the second cake layer and spread with the same amount of frosting. Top with the third cake layer and generously frost the top and sides of the cake with the remaining frosting, smoothing it evenly with an offset spatula or bench scraper. Encrust the top and sides of the cake completely with the candied walnuts, pressing them gently into the icing to help them stick. Refrigerate the cake until firm, at least 1 to 2 hours. The cake can be refrigerated for up to 24 hours before serving.

Remove the cake from the refrigerator 1 to 2 hours before slicing and serving. Store the cake in a covered cake carrier or other container in the refrigerator for up to 3 days.

FRENCH MERINGUE KISSES

3 egg whites, at room temperature

¼ tsp cream of tartar

½ cup [100 g] superfine granulated sugar

⅛ tsp fine sea salt

½ tsp vanilla extract

½ cup [60 g] confectioners' sugar, sifted

LEMON CURD

1½ cups [300 g] granulated sugar

Grated zest of 3 lemons

4 eggs

4 egg yolks (reserve 3 of the egg whites to make the French Meringues Kisses, above)

¾ cup [180 ml] freshly squeezed lemon juice

¾ cup [165 g] unsalted butter, cut into 8 pieces, at room temperature

LEMON CAKE

2¾ cups [550 g] granulated sugar

2 Tbsp grated lemon zest

2¾ cups [385 g] all-purpose flour

3 tsp baking powder

1 tsp fine sea salt

4 eggs, at room temperature

1¼ cups [300 ml] canola oil

1 tsp vanilla extract

2 Tbsp freshly squeezed lemon juice

1 cup [240 ml] whole milk, at room temperature

LIMONCELLO SYRUP

1 cup [200 g] granulated sugar

⅔ cup [160 ml] freshly squeezed lemon juice

¼ cup [60 ml] limoncello

LEMON BOMB BUTTERCREAM

6 eggs

2 cups [400 g] granulated sugar

3 cups [680 g] unsalted butter, at room temperature

1 Tbsp freshly squeezed lemon juice

1 tsp vanilla extract

⅛ tsp fine sea salt

½ to ¾ cup [120 g to 180 g] Lemon Curd (from above)

Confectioners' sugar for sprinkling

Citrus lovers will stop in their tracks for this lovely and impressive lemon cake. The layers are brushed with a simple syrup spiked with limoncello, a lemon liqueur from southern Italy made with the zest of Sorrento lemons, which are famous for their intense perfume. I've encrusted the entire cake with crumbled chunks of crisp French meringue for a little crunch. Feel free to purchase meringue cookies from your favorite bakery or specialty shop if you don't want to bake your own.

LEMON BOMB

SERVES 8 TO 10

TO MAKE THE MERINGUE KISSES: Preheat the oven to 200°F [95°C]. Line a baking sheet with parchment paper.

In a stand mixer fitted with the whisk attachment, beat the egg whites with the cream of tartar on low speed until foamy. Add the salt, increase the mixer speed to medium-high, and continue beating until soft peaks form. Continue beating while adding the superfine sugar, 1 tablespoon at a time, until stiff, glossy peaks form. Beat in the vanilla. Sift the confectioners' sugar a second time over the meringue and, using a rubber or silicone spatula, fold in just until no streaks of sugar remain, taking care not to deflate the egg whites.

Spoon the meringue in 2-in [5-cm] free-form dollops at least 1 in [2.5 cm] apart onto the prepared baking sheet.

Bake until crisp and dry, about 3 hours. Turn the oven off and leave the meringues in the oven for about 1 hour longer to cool thoroughly. (The meringues can be made up to 1 week in advance and stored

at room temperature in a tightly covered container.)

TO MAKE THE LEMON CURD: Put the sugar in a 2-quart stainless steel or pyrex bowl, add the lemon zest, and rub the sugar and lemon zest together with your fingertips until the sugar is moist and sandy and fragrant with lemon. Whisk in the eggs, egg yolks, and lemon juice.

Set the bowl over (but not touching) a simmering saucepan of water to form a double boiler. Whisk continuously over simmering water until the mixture becomes smooth and creamy, and thickens enough to thickly coat the back of a wooden spoon. Remove the pan from the heat and whisk in the softened butter, 1 Tbsp at a time. Continue whisking just until the lemon curd is smooth.

Set a fine-mesh sieve over a clean bowl and strain the lemon curd through the sieve into the bowl. Cover the lemon curd with plastic wrap, pressing it onto the surface to prevent a skin from forming. Refrigerate until very cold, 3 to 4 hours

Continued

and preferably overnight. (The lemon curd can be made up to 3 days ahead and stored, tightly covered, in the refrigerator.

Position a rack in the center of the oven. Preheat the oven to 350°F [180°C]. Coat three 8-in [20-cm] or 9-in [23-cm] round cake pans with nonstick cooking spray and line the bottoms with parchment paper.

TO MAKE THE CAKE: In a small bowl, rub the sugar and lemon zest together with your fingertips, until the sugar is moist and sandy and fragrant with lemon. Set aside.

In a medium bowl, sift together the flour, baking powder, and salt. Set aside.

In a stand mixer fitted with the whisk attachment, beat the eggs and lemon sugar at medium-high speed until light, fluffy, and doubled in volume, 4 to 5 minutes. With the mixer running, slowly drizzle in the oil until the mixture is thick and emulsified. Beat in the vanilla and lemon juice. Stop the mixer and scrape down the sides of the bowl, if needed.

With the mixer on low, add the dry ingredients to the batter in three additions, alternating with the milk in two additions, beating just until combined, 15 to 20 seconds after each.

Divide the batter evenly between the pans and spread the tops smooth with a spatula. Bake for 22 to 28 minutes, until a wooden skewer inserted into the center of each cake comes out clean. Transfer to wire racks to cool for 10 minutes. Invert the cakes onto the racks and discard the parchment paper.

TO MAKE THE LIMONCELLO SYRUP: Combine the sugar and lemon juice in

a small saucepan. Cook over medium heat, stirring occasionally, until the sugar dissolves and the mixture comes to a boil. Decrease the heat to low and simmer until syrupy, 2 to 3 minutes. Remove from the heat and stir in the limoncello.

While the cakes are still warm, brush each layer generously with the warm syrup and let it soak in. Let the cakes cool completely.

TO MAKE THE BUTTERCREAM: Fill a large sauté pan with water and bring to a simmer over medium heat. Combine the eggs and sugar in the bowl of a stand mixer and place the bowl in the pan of simmering water. Using a large balloon whisk, whisk together the eggs and sugar continuously (do not stop or the eggs might scramble) until the sugar is completely dissolved and the mixture is very thick and fluffy and hot to the touch, 3 to 5 minutes. It should register between 120° and 140°F [50° and 60°C] on an instant-read candy thermometer.

Remove the bowl from the simmering water and, using the whisk attachment on the stand mixer, beat the egg mixture at high speed until it triples in volume, forms soft peaks, and the bottom of the bowl is cool to the touch, 10 to 13 minutes.

Decrease the speed to medium and gradually beat in the softened butter, 2 Tbsp at a time, beating well after each addition. (Don't panic if the buttercream starts to liquefy or look curdled as you beat in the butter. It will magically emulsify into a smooth, silky frosting by the time the last bit of butter has been added. Trust me.) Beat in the lemon juice, vanilla, and salt, just until incorporated.

When the buttercream is smooth and glossy, remove the bowl from the mixer and fold in ½ cup [120 g] of the lemon curd by hand with a rubber or silicone spatula.

TO FINISH THE CAKE: Fit a large disposable piping bag with a large round tip. Fill the bag halfway with buttercream.

Place one cake layer on a cardboard cake board, cake plate, or cake stand.

Spread the cake layer with a thin layer of buttercream. Pipe a rope of buttercream around the edge of the cake to form a dam to hold the lemon curd and prevent it from leaking out. Fill the center with about ¾ cup [180 g] of lemon curd and top with the next cake layer. Spread with more buttercream, create another buttercream dam, and fill with more lemon curd. Top with the final cake layer. Refrigerate the cake for 15 to 30 minutes to set the filling before continuing to frost.

Spread the top and sides of the chilled cake with a thin layer of buttercream to form a crumb coat (see page 21). Refrigerate until the buttercream is very firm, 15 to 30 minutes. Spread the remaining buttercream smoothly over the top and sides of the cake.

Coarsely crumble half the meringues with your fingers and press thickly around the sides of the cake. Break the remaining meringues into larger chunks and mound onto the top of the cake. Sift confectioners' sugar lightly over the top of the cake. The cake can sit, uncovered at room temperature, for up to 4 hours.

If you have never tasted iced hibiscus tea, or *agua de Jamaica*, as it is called throughout Mexico, you are in for a treat. I discovered it for myself at a tiny taco stand in San Diego. Immediately enchanted with its rich ruby color and invigorating tartness, I couldn't wait to make it for myself at home. The tea is made from dark red dried hibiscus blossoms, also known as *flor de Jamaica*, and it's no more difficult to make than a cup of Earl Grey. Steep dried blossoms in hot water with fresh ginger, add lime juice, and then sweeten with a little sugar. For a fun hybrid between a Latin American *tres leches* cake and a kitschy American Jell-O poke cake, I simmer the sweet hibiscus tea until it's syrupy, and then set it with gelatin before pouring it over delicate layers of lime chiffon cake. It's cool, tart, and refreshing, with a subtle, gingery bite.

THE HIBISCUS

SERVES 8 TO 10

LIME CHIFFON CAKE
2 cups [200 g] sifted cake flour
1¾ cups [350 g] sugar
2 tsp baking powder
½ tsp fine sea salt
6 eggs, at room temperature
½ cup [120 ml] vegetable oil
½ cup [120 ml] water
¼ cup [60 ml] freshly squeezed lime juice
1 tsp grated lime zest
1 tsp vanilla extract
½ tsp cream of tartar

HIBISCUS-GINGER-LIME SYRUP
1½ cups [360 ml] water
1 cup [60 g] dried hibiscus flowers
One 2-in [5-cm] chunk fresh ginger, peeled and coarsely chopped
5 tsp unflavored granulated gelatin
1 cup [200 g] sugar
½ cup [120 ml] freshly squeezed lime juice

TOPPING
1½ cups [360 ml] chilled heavy cream
½ cup [120 g] chilled crème fraîche
¼ cup [50 g] sugar, plus more if needed
2 Tbsp freshly squeezed lime juice

¼ cup [35 g] finely minced candied ginger
Thin lime slices for decorating

Position a rack in the center of the oven. Preheat the oven to 325°F [165°C]. Lightly grease the bottoms of two 9-in [23-cm] round cake pans and line the bottoms with parchment paper. Do not grease the sides of the pan.

TO MAKE THE CAKE: Sift together the flour, 1¼ cups [250 g] of the sugar, the baking powder, and the salt into a large bowl. Set aside.

Separate 5 of the eggs. Put the 5 egg whites in the bowl of a stand mixer and set aside.

Place the 5 egg yolks in a medium bowl. Using a large balloon whisk, beat the egg yolks together by hand with the remaining whole egg, the oil, water, lime juice and zest, and vanilla until thick and smooth, about 1 minute. Make a well in the center of the dry ingredients and scrape the wet ingredients into the well. Beat together with a hand mixer set at medium speed until thick and smooth, 1 to 2 minutes.

In a stand mixer fitted with the whisk attachment, beat the egg whites and cream of tartar on low until soft peaks form. With the mixer still running, add the remaining ½ cup [100 g] sugar to the egg whites, 1 tablespoon at a time, until they are fluffy and light and hold firm peaks when the beaters are lifted from the bowl.

Using a rubber or silicone spatula, gently fold one-third of the egg whites into the cake batter to lighten it. Fold in the remaining whites just until blended, taking care not to deflate them or to overmix the batter.

Divide the batter between the prepared pans and smooth the tops with a spatula. Bake for 20 to 25 minutes, until the cake

Continued

springs back when lightly touched with a finger and a wooden skewer inserted into the center of each cake comes out clean. Invert the pans onto a wire rack, allowing the cake layers to cool completely while they are upside down (do not remove the pans). When the layers are cool, run a thin, offset spatula around the edges of each cake to loosen from the pan. Carefully remove the cake layers from the pan and peel off the parchment paper.

TO MAKE THE SYRUP: In a 2-qt [2-L] saucepan, combine the water, hibiscus flowers, and ginger and bring to a boil over medium-high heat. Decrease the heat to low and simmer until the water is a deep red, about 10 minutes. Remove from the heat and cover. Let cool completely. Strain through a fine-mesh sieve into a small bowl, pressing the hibiscus flowers to extract all the liquid. Discard the flowers and ginger. Transfer ⅓ cup [80 ml] of the cooled hibiscus tea to another small bowl and sprinkle it with the gelatin. Let it stand for a few minutes to soften.

Combine the remaining hibiscus tea and the sugar in a 2-qt [2-L] saucepan over medium heat, bring to a boil, and stir until the sugar is dissolved. Decrease the heat to medium-low and simmer until lightly syrupy, 3 to 5 minutes. Add the lime juice and gelatin mixture, stirring just until the gelatin is dissolved. Pour the mixture into a measuring cup with a spout and let cool to room temperature.

Line two clean 9-in [23-cm] round cake pans with plastic wrap. Place the cake layers back in the cake pans, top-side up. With the fat end of a chopstick, pierce both layers all over the top, halfway through the cake. Pour half of the hibiscus syrup over each layer. Refrigerate for at least 3 to 4 hours and preferably overnight, until the cakes are very cold and the gelatin is firm.

TO MAKE THE TOPPING: An hour or two before serving, chill the bowl and whisk attachment from a stand mixer for 15 minutes. Beat together the heavy cream, crème fraîche, and sugar on medium speed until soft, mounding peaks form. With the mixer running, beat in the lime juice. Taste for sweetness, adding more sugar if needed, 1 tablespoon at a time, until the topping has the sweetness you like.

Grasping the plastic wrap, pull each cake layer from their pans. Carefully ease the first layer onto a cake stand or cake plate, discarding the plastic wrap. Spread with about one-third of the whipped-cream topping. Top with the second layer of cake and frost the tops and sides of the cake with the remaining topping. Sprinkle the top of the cake with the minced candied ginger and lime slices. Cover lightly with plastic wrap and refrigerate until ready to serve. The cake is best served within 2 hours of being frosted, but will keep, covered and refrigerated, for up to 2 days.

My head is so often turned by flashier cakes full of chocolate or caramel, I sometimes forget how comforting it is to bake an old-fashioned spice cake like gingerbread. The strong, sweet perfume of molasses, ginger, and cloves as it envelops my kitchen is intoxicating. If any scent conjures the ideal of a happy childhood, I think it is the melting aroma of butter, sugar, and spices like cinnamon, nutmeg, and cloves mingling and merging to flavor a simple apple cake or the perfect pumpkin pie.

The only thing better than a comforting spice cake is one made a bit boozy with a drop or two of dark rum or a rich, sweet slug of good bourbon. Cakes sweetened with brown sugar or molasses shine a little bit brighter with a splash of spirits stirred into the batter.

SPIRITS & SPICES BASICS

LITTLE BOTTLES

I love baking and experimenting with lots of different spirits and liqueurs, and I always stock bourbon, dark rum, and brandy in my pantry for baking. But when I have an urge to experiment with something more exotic or unusual, I don't always want to make the investment in a big bottle if I only need a few tablespoons. So I buy little 50-ml bottles (just like the cute little bottles they serve on airplanes). I can get almost anything I want in these small sizes, and it is an inexpensive way to satisfy my curiosity. The first time I tried St. Germain, the French liqueur distilled from handpicked elderflowers, I bought it in a little bottle. It turned out this elixir is wonderful with berries and tropical fruits, and worth the splurge to invest in a larger bottle. I have a collection of little bottles of spiced and coconut rums, crème de banane for the next time I have a craving for Bananas Foster, honey whiskey liqueur, many different eau de vie, like kirschwasser and pear brandy. I once brought home little bottles of Irish whiskey, bourbon, and rye whiskey for an unofficial tasting to determine my favorite. There's even a little bottle of Fireball Cinnamon Whisky in my cupboard to crack open in case of emergencies.

SPICES

For thousands of years, spices were prized for more than just their heavenly aroma and flavor. Crusaders and pilgrims to the Holy Land were introduced to many spices by Arab traders, who kept the origins of their spice routes as secret as possible, conjuring fantastical tales of dragons and sea serpents to discourage curious Europeans from discovering their sources in Asia and Africa. Rare and expensive black pepper, cardamom, ginger, cinnamon, cloves, and especially nutmeg were touted for their abilities to preserve food, as well as for medicinal and curative properties. Black pepper was worth more than gold. Nutmeg was thought to cure everything from the common cold and stomach ailments to bad breath and impotence—and even the plague. The Vikings became enamored with the heady fragrance of cardamom, a spice native to India and Sri Lanka, after sampling it during their many raids on Constantinople in Turkey, then a bridge for goods flowing between Asia and Europe. They carried the exotic and aromatic cardamom pods home, and it is still Scandinavia's most beloved spice, used liberally in their many recipes for cakes and breads, cookies, and pastries. In the early 1500s, the seafaring Portuguese explorers, and later Dutch and English traders, battled fiercely to control the tiny and remote Moluccas—also known as the Spice Islands—in Indonesia, then the only known location of nutmeg and clove trees. The competition for nutmeg was so great between the English and the Dutch that in order to quell hostilities between the two nations, the English agreed to forgo any rights to the tiny spice island of Run, then lush and overgrown with nutmeg trees, in exchange for a few colonies across the sea—which included the island of Manhattan.

In medieval Europe, adding spices became the norm when cooking the more extravagant foods and sweets eaten during the winter solstice—and later, Christmas celebrations. German monks became famous for their *lebkuchen*, or spiced honey cakes. Today the warm aroma of gingerbread made with cinnamon, ginger, cloves, and nutmeg is the iconic fragrance of Christmas.

Hefeweizen is a lovely, crisp, wheat beer brewed with coriander, cloves, and a dash of orange zest. It makes a flavorful base for this unusual spice cake. Coriander is customarily seen in savory dishes, but it has a bright, citrusy tang that marries well with the honey and orange flavors in this golden loaf.

BIG HONEY HEFEWEIZEN SPICE CAKE

SERVES 6 TO 8

Position a rack in the center of the oven. Preheat the oven to 325°F [165°C]. Coat a 9-by-5-in [23-by-12-cm] metal loaf pan with nonstick cooking spray. Line the pan with an 8½-by-15-in [21.5-by-38-cm] strip of parchment paper so it covers the bottom of the pan and hangs over the long sides.

In a medium bowl, sift together the flour, baking powder, salt, coriander, nutmeg, allspice, and cloves. Set aside.

In a medium saucepan, combine the beer, honey, butter, and grated zest. Heat over medium heat, stirring occasionally, until the butter melts. Increase the heat to medium-high, bring the beer mixture to a boil, and cook for 1 to 2 minutes. Remove from the heat and let cool to lukewarm.

In a medium bowl, beat together the eggs and sugar with an electric mixer set at medium-high speed until pale and thick, 3 to 4 minutes. Add the dry ingredients to the bowl in three additions, alternating with the beer mixture in two additions and beating just until smooth. Do not overmix or the cake will be tough.

Scrape the batter into the prepared pan and bake for 45 to 55 minutes, until a wooden skewer inserted into the center of the cake comes out clean.

Set the pan to cool on a wire rack for 10 minutes. Grasping the overhanging parchment, lift the loaf out of the pan and set it on the rack. Let cool completely before glazing. Discard the parchment paper.

TO MAKE THE GLAZE: In a medium bowl, whisk the melted butter and zest together until well combined. Whisk in the confectioners' sugar and the juice until the glaze is thick and creamy but still pourable.

Drizzle the glaze over the cake, allowing it to drip down the sides. Let set before slicing. The cake will keep, well wrapped in plastic wrap at room temperature, for up to 3 days.

2 cups [280 g] all-purpose flour

2 tsp baking powder

½ tsp fine sea salt

½ tsp ground coriander

½ tsp freshly grated nutmeg

½ tsp ground allspice

⅛ tsp ground cloves

¾ cup [180 ml] hefeweizen beer, preferably one brewed with honey

⅓ cup [115 ml] mild honey, preferably orange blossom

½ cup [110 g] unsalted butter, cut into 8 pieces

1 tsp grated clementine or orange zest

2 eggs

1 cup [200 g] granulated sugar

CLEMENTINE GLAZE

1 Tbsp unsalted butter, melted

½ tsp grated clementine or orange zest

1 cup [120 g] confectioners' sugar

2 Tbsp fresh clementine or orange juice

I have witnessed the awesome power of a good crumb cake. It was the beginning of my daughter Sophia's softball season, and the other team was bigger, more experienced, and seemed to have arms made of steel. Bats were swung and bases missed. Our girls played hard, but they still lost. As they walked off the field, hot, dusty, and a little blue, I lifted the lid off my trusty traveling treat carrier. It was filled with big squares of cinnamon crumb cake, rich and moist, each piece topped with a heaping mound of brown sugar crumble. I felt like a superhero. The coaches hugged me, the girls started giggling, the parents smiled. It was a good day—for softball and crumb cake.

CRUMB TOPPING

2 cups [400 g] firmly packed dark brown sugar

2¼ cups [315 g] all-purpose flour

2 tsp ground cinnamon

¼ tsp baking powder

¼ teaspoon fine sea salt

1 cup [220 g] unsalted butter, melted

CAKE BATTER

2 cups [280 g] all-purpose flour

1¼ tsp baking powder

½ tsp baking soda

1 tsp fine sea salt

¾ cup [165 g] unsalted butter, at room temperature

1 cup [200 g] granulated sugar

2 eggs

2 tsp vanilla extract

1 cup [240 g] sour cream

Confectioners' sugar for sprinkling

CLASSIC DINER CRUMB CAKE

SERVES 12

Position a rack in the center of the oven. Preheat the oven to 350°F [180°C]. Coat a 9-by-13-in [23-by-33 cm] baking pan with nonstick cooking spray.

TO MAKE THE TOPPING: In a medium bowl, stir together the brown sugar, flour, cinnamon, baking powder, and salt. Add the melted butter and stir with a fork until the butter is absorbed and the mixture is crumbly. To get big, chunky pieces, grab handfuls of crumbs and compress them together, then break these larger nuggets into slightly smaller pieces to scatter over the batter before baking. Set aside.

TO MAKE THE CAKE: Sift together the flour, baking powder, baking soda, and salt into a medium bowl. Set aside.

In the bowl of a stand mixer fitted with the paddle attachment, beat the butter and sugar together at medium speed until light and fluffy, 3 to 4 minutes. Beat in the eggs, one at a time, beating well after each addition, then beat in the vanilla and sour cream. Scrape down the sides of the bowl. Add the dry ingredients and beat on low speed just until combined.

Scrape the batter into the prepared pan, smoothing the top with a spatula. Using your hands, sprinkle the topping evenly over the batter, making sure some of the larger clumps remain as you go and covering the top completely.

Bake for 30 to 35 minutes, until a wooden skewer inserted into the center of the cake comes out clean and the crumb topping is firm. Transfer to a wire rack and let cool for 10 to 15 minutes. Sprinkle with confectioners' sugar. Cut into squares and serve. The cake will keep, tightly covered at room temperature, for up to 2 days.

My maternal grandmother wasn't much of a cook. "All that work and it's gone in fifteen minutes," she would say. She preferred to sew or quilt, and couldn't believe I once took a coat to the dry cleaners to sew on a loose button. I imagine she would like this rich and spicy gingerbread cake—it's bold and aromatic, sweet but with a peppery kick, and, best of all, it's very easy to make. I particularly love using cultured butter, especially Irish butter, in this cake; it's denser and creamier than ordinary butter, with a higher milk-fat content and a richer, more complex flavor. A compote of sliced apples sautéed in more Irish butter, brown sugar, and a shot of good Irish whiskey makes a lovely accompaniment.

MY PRETEND IRISH GRANDMA'S
IRISH WHISKEY GINGERBREAD

SERVES 10 TO 12

2½ cups [350 g] all-purpose flour

1½ tsp baking powder

1 tsp fine sea salt

5 tsp ground ginger

2 tsp ground cinnamon

½ tsp freshly grated nutmeg

¼ tsp ground allspice

¼ tsp finely ground white pepper

1 cup [240 ml] ginger beer
(I like Fever-Tree ginger beer)

1¼ cups [400 g] molasses

1 cup [220 g] unsalted cultured butter, preferably Irish butter

1 cup [200 g] firmly packed dark brown sugar

¾ cup [150 g] granulated sugar

1 tsp instant espresso powder or instant coffee granules

1½ tsp baking soda

3 eggs

3 Tbsp Irish whiskey

½ cup [120 ml] buttermilk

One 2-in [5-cm] chunk fresh ginger, peeled and grated on a Microplane zester

Confectioners' sugar for sprinkling

Position a rack in the center of the oven. Preheat the oven to 350°F [180°C]. Coat a 10- or 12-cup [2.4- or 2.8 L] Bundt pan with nonstick cooking spray.

Sift together the flour, baking powder, salt, ground ginger, cinnamon, nutmeg, cloves, and pepper in a large bowl. Set aside.

In a medium 3-qt [3-L] saucepan, combine the ginger beer, molasses, butter, brown sugar, granulated sugar, and espresso powder. Stir over medium heat until the butter melts, the sugars dissolve, and the mixture is very hot.

Remove from the heat and stir in the baking soda. The baking soda will fizz and bubble as it hits the warm syrup. Stir with a wooden spoon until the bubbling subsides. Whisk in the eggs, one at a time. Stir in the whiskey, buttermilk, and fresh ginger.

Make a well in the center of the dry ingredients and add the warm ginger-beer mixture. Use a whisk to gently fold the ingredients into a smooth batter.

Scrape the batter into the prepared pan and bake for 30 to 35 minutes, until a wooden skewer inserted into the center of the cake comes out clean.

Transfer to a wire rack and let cool for 10 minutes. Unmold onto a serving platter and sprinkle with confectioners' sugar before slicing and serving.

Store in a covered cake carrier at room temperature for up to 2 days.

CROWD-PLEASER

If I were a pirate with a sweet tooth, this might be the cake I would spirit away with me on long sea voyages. Nutty, dense, moist, and aromatic with dark rum and brown butter, this flavorful cake is also scented with cardamom and nutmeg—spices once valued more than gold. It gets better and more complex as it ages.

THE BUCCANEER

SERVES 10 TO 12, IN SMALL SLIVERS

MUSCOVADO SUGAR SYRUP

1½ cups [300 g] firmly packed dark muscovado sugar or dark brown sugar

¾ cup [180 ml] water

CAKE BATTER

2 cups [280 g] all-purpose flour

1¾ tsp baking powder

¼ tsp baking soda

¾ tsp fine sea salt

1½ tsp ground cinnamon

1 tsp ground ginger

½ tsp ground cardamom

½ tsp freshly grated nutmeg

¾ cup [90 g] finely ground almonds or almond meal

¾ cup [165 g] unsalted butter, plus 2 Tbsp

1 cup [200 g] granulated sugar

3 eggs

¾ cup [180 ml] buttermilk

5 Tbsp [75 ml] dark rum

2 tsp vanilla extract

TO MAKE THE SYRUP: In a 3-qt [3-L] stainless-steel saucepan, stir together the sugar and water. Simmer over medium heat, stirring until the sugar dissolves. Increase the heat to medium-high and bring the syrup to a boil. Cook, stirring occasionally, until the syrup thickens to the consistency of maple syrup, 4 to 5 minutes. Remove from the heat and let cool completely. (If making ahead, store the syrup in a covered container in the refrigerator for up to 1 week.)

TO MAKE THE CAKE: Position a rack in the center of the oven. Preheat the oven to 350°F [180°C]. Coat a 9-in [23-cm] round cake pan with 3-in [7.5-cm] sides with nonstick cooking spray and line with parchment paper.

In a medium bowl, sift together the flour, baking powder, baking soda, salt, cinnamon, ginger, cardamom, and nutmeg. Whisk in the ground almonds and set aside.

Melt the ¾ cup [165 g] butter in a medium stainless-steel saucepan over low heat. Increase the heat to high and bring the butter to a boil. Continue cooking, stirring often, until the milk solids at the bottom

of the pan begin to brown. The butter will develop a sweet, nutty aroma—this should take 5 to 7 minutes. Pour the butter and all the browned bits into a large bowl to stop any further browning. Whisk in the granulated sugar, ¾ cup [180 ml] of the Muscovado Sugar Syrup, the eggs, buttermilk, 3 Tbsp of the dark rum, and the vanilla. Fold the dry ingredients into the batter by hand using a rubber or silicone spatula, just until combined. Do not overmix.

Scrape the batter into the prepared pan, spreading the top evenly with a spatula. Bake for 45 to 55 minutes, until a wooden skewer inserted into the center of the cake comes out clean. Transfer to a wire rack and let cool completely in the pan. Invert cake onto the rack and peel off the parchment paper. Place another rack over the cake, invert again, and place the rack on a rimmed baking sheet (to catch any drips when you glaze the cake).

TO FINISH THE CAKE: In a medium saucepan, bring ½ cup [120 ml] of the Muscovado Sugar Syrup and the 2 Tbsp butter to a boil over medium-high heat. Decrease the heat to low and simmer the syrup about 2 minutes. Remove from the heat and stir in the remaining 2 Tbsp dark rum.

Brush the glaze over the top and sides of the cake, letting it soak in before brushing on more. Keep brushing the glaze over the top and sides of the cake until it is completely absorbed. As the glaze cools, it will crystallize into a dark, glossy sheen. When the cake is completely glazed and cool, store it in a covered container at room temperature until ready to serve. This cake is best served the day after it's made, and will keep, tightly covered, for up to 3 days at room temperature.

2 cups [280 g] all-purpose flour

2 tsp baking soda

2 tsp ground cinnamon

¾ tsp fine sea salt

1 cup [240 ml] canola or vegetable oil

1¼ cups [250 g] granulated sugar

2 eggs

1 tsp vanilla extract

2 cups [600 g] fig jam

1 cup [240 ml] boiling water

1½ cups [180 g] chopped walnuts, toasted
(see page 16)

BRANDIED HARD SAUCE ICING

1 cup [165 g] unsalted butter, at room
temperature

4 to 5 cups [480 to 600 g] confectioners'
sugar

Pinch of fine sea salt

¼ tsp vanilla extract

3 to 4 Tbsp brandy

Freshly grated nutmeg for sprinkling

It's a truth universally acknowledged: If you spend your college years saturated in Jane Austen and Charles Dickens, you are likely to develop a fascination for English desserts like Jam Roly-Poly, Dundee cake, and Victoria sponge. This rich, sticky fig cake is my homage to figgy pudding (which actually contains no figs), complete with an icing inspired by a classic hard sauce to slather on top. Make sure to use proper jam, and not fig spread—fig jam is made from fresh figs and sugar, whereas fig spread is made from puréed and lightly sweetened dried figs. The spread is thicker and heavier than jam, with a denser texture that would overwhelm this cake.

TIPSY FIG CAKE
WITH BRANDIED HARD SAUCE ICING

SERVES 8

Position a rack in the center of the oven. Preheat the oven to 350°F [180°C]. Coat two 8-in [20-cm] round or square cake pans with nonstick cooking spray and line the bottoms with parchment paper.

Sift together the flour, baking soda, cinnamon, and salt into a medium bowl. Set aside.

In a large bowl, using an electric hand mixer set at medium speed, beat together the oil, sugar, eggs, and vanilla until thick and creamy. On low speed, beat in the fig jam. Add the dry ingredients, one-third at a time, beating 10 to 15 seconds after each addition, just until smooth and combined. Add the boiling water to the batter, beating just until smooth. Fold in the walnuts.

Divide the batter evenly between the prepared pans, smoothing the tops with a spatula. Bake for 30 to 35 minutes, until a wooden skewer inserted into the center of each cake comes out clean.

Transfer the cakes to wire racks and let cool completely in their pans. Invert the layers onto the racks and discard the parchment paper. At this point, the cake can be frosted and served, but if you have the will power to resist, it is even better if allowed to age at room temperature for at least 1 day for the flavors to ripen. Wrap the layers separately in plastic wrap and let them sit at room temperature for up to 2 days before frosting and serving.

Continued

TO MAKE THE ICING: In a stand mixer fitted with the paddle attachment, beat the butter at medium speed until creamy, about 2 minutes. Sift 3 cups [360 g] of the confectioners' sugar and beat into the butter until fluffy. Beat in the vanilla and then the brandy, 1 Tbsp at a time, adding as much brandy as the icing can absorb while remaining very thick and creamy, but still spreadable. If the icing becomes too thin, beat in the remaining sifted confectioners' sugar.

Set one layer on a cake plate or cake stand and spread the top with half the icing. Top with the second cake layer and spread the remaining icing evenly over the top of the cake, leaving the sides of the cake naked. Grate a little fresh nutmeg over the surface of the cake. Store in a covered cake carrier or other container at room temperature for up to 2 days.

For this spectacular cake, I took the iconic marshmallow-topped sweet potato casserole and turned it into a glorious towering dessert: six layers of spicy sweet potato cake sandwiched with a rich, buttery praline filling and swathed in a glossy cloud of burnished marshmallow meringue. I like to use garnet yams (which are, in fact, sweet potatoes and not yams, just to confuse you). Their bright orange flesh is dense, moist, and subtly sweet. This cake is particularly fun to serve after Thanksgiving dinner. You can make the cake layers and freeze them up to 2 weeks ahead of time. Fill and frost the cake the morning of the big event.

SWEET POTATO-PRALINE SPICE CAKE
WITH MARSHMALLOW MERINGUE

SERVES 8 TO 10

3 cups [420 g] all-purpose flour

2 tsp baking powder

1 tsp baking soda

1¼ tsp fine sea salt

4 tsp ground cinnamon

1 tsp ground ginger

1 tsp ground allspice

½ tsp freshly grated nutmeg

½ tsp ground cloves

2 medium sweet potatoes such as garnet yams (see recipe introduction)

4 eggs

1½ cups [300 g] firmly packed dark brown sugar

1 cup [200 g] granulated sugar

¾ cup [180 ml] buttermilk

½ cup plus 2 Tbsp [140 g] unsalted butter, melted

½ cup [120 ml] canola or vegetable oil

3 Tbsp bourbon, dark rum, or cognac

2 tsp vanilla extract

BROWN BUTTER-PRALINE FILLING

1 cup [220 g] unsalted butter, at room temperature

2 cups [400 g] firmly packed dark brown sugar

2 Tbsp Golden Syrup (see page 17) or dark corn syrup

2 Tbsp bourbon, dark rum, or Cognac

1⅓ cups [320 ml] heavy cream

½ teaspoon fine sea salt

3 cups [360 g] confectioners' sugar, sifted

1½ tsp vanilla extract

MARSHMALLOW MERINGUE

3 egg whites

1½ cups [300 g] granulated sugar

½ cup [170 ml] light corn syrup

¼ cup [60 ml] water

1½ tsp vanilla extract

Position a rack in the center of the oven. Preheat the oven to 375°F [190°C]. Coat three 8-in [20-cm] round cake pans with nonstick cooking spray and line the bottoms with parchment paper.

Sift together the flour, baking powder, baking soda, salt, cinnamon, ginger, allspice, nutmeg, and cloves into a medium bowl. Set aside.

Prick the sweet potatoes all over with a fork and bake on a rimmed baking sheet until they are very tender when pierced with a knife, about 1 hour. Remove from the oven and let cool completely. Halve the potatoes, scoop the flesh into a bowl, and mash with a fork. Measure 2 packed cups [460 g] of the flesh into a food processor fitted with the metal blade and pulse until smooth.

Add the eggs and sugars to the food processor and pulse to combine. Pour the buttermilk, melted butter, oil, bourbon, and vanilla through the feeding tube, processing with a few short pulses, just until smooth.

Continued

Remove the top of the processor and scrape down the sides. Add the dry ingredients and give the processor a few final pulses until the batter is smooth. Divide the batter evenly between the prepared pans and smooth the tops with a spatula. Tap the pans once or twice on the counter to settle the batter.

Bake for 30 to 35 minutes, until a wooden skewer inserted into the center of each cake comes out with just a few moist crumbs clinging to it. Let the cake layers cool in their pans on wire racks for 10 minutes, and then invert them onto the racks. Discard the parchment paper. Let cool completely before frosting.

TO MAKE THE BROWN BUTTER-PRALINE FILLING: Melt ¾ cup [170 g] of the butter in a medium saucepan over low heat. When the butter is melted, increase the heat to medium-high and bring to a boil, stirring constantly. As the butter boils, it will snap and sizzle and sound like distant applause or frying bacon. As the water in the butter burns off, the sizzling will slowly die down, and that is when the milk solids in the butter will start to brown and develop a sweet and nutty aroma. Stir constantly, scraping up the browned bits on the bottom of the pan, and to ensure the butter browns evenly, 3 to 5 minutes.

Remove from the heat and immediately stir in the brown sugar, golden syrup, bourbon, and cream. Return the pan to the heat and cook, stirring occasionally, until the sugar dissolves. Bring to a boil and cook for exactly 2 minutes. (Set a timer!) Remove from the heat and scrape into the bowl of a stand mixer fitted with the paddle attachment. With the mixer on low speed, beat in the sifted confectioners' sugar. Continue beating until the frosting is thick and creamy and the mixer bowl is cool to the touch, 5 to 6 minues. Beat in the remaining 4 Tbsp [60 g] room temperature butter, 1 Tbsp at a time, until fully incorporated.

With a long, serrated bread knife, cut each cake layer in half horizontally (see page 21). Place one layer, cut-side up, on a cake plate or cake stand. Spread one-fifth of the praline filling over the top of the cake, pushing it to the edges. Top with a second layer, cut-side down. Continue frosting and stacking the remaining cake layers. Top with the final layer of cake, cut-side down.

TO MAKE THE MARSHMALLOW MERINGUE: In a stand mixer fitted with the whisk attachment, beat the egg whites on medium speed until soft peaks form, 3 to 4 minutes.

In a 3-qt [3-L] saucepan, stir the sugar, corn syrup, and water together until well blended. Over medium heat, bring to a rolling boil, covered. Uncover and boil 4 to 8 minutes, without stirring, until the syrup reaches 242°F [116°C] on an instant-read candy thermometer (tip the pan to one side so the syrup is deep enough for the thermometer to accurately measure the temperature), or until ½ tsp of the syrup dropped into cup of ice water forms a soft, malleable ball (see page 91). With the mixer on medium speed, slowly pour the hot syrup in a thin, steady stream into egg whites, beating constantly. Add the vanilla. Increase the mixer speed to high and continue beating for 8 to 10 minutes, until the meringue is stiff and glossy, but still warm.

Using a rubber or silicone spatula, scrape all the meringue onto the top of the cake. With an offset spatula, quickly spread the marshmallow meringue thickly over the top and sides of the cake. Use the spatula or the back of a spoon to create swirls and spikes all over the cake. At this point, the cake can sit at room temperature up to 8 hours before browning the meringue.

TO FINISH THE CAKE: Right before serving, use a propane blowtorch or butane kitchen torch to lightly brown the meringue: Hold the torch 2 to 3 inches from the cake, waving the flame over the meringue to caramelize it lightly. Serve immediately, slicing the cake into thin wedges with a long, thin knife. Any leftovers can be stored in a covered cake carrier at room temperature for 1 more day.

TENNESSEE WHISKEY SYRUP

½ cup [100 g] granulated sugar

¼ cup [60 ml] water

4 Tbsp unsalted butter

¼ cup [60 ml] Tennessee whiskey (such as Jack Daniel's or George Dickel) or bourbon, if you prefer

CAKE BATTER

2¾ cups [385 g] all-purpose flour

3 tsp baking powder

¼ tsp baking soda

1 tsp fine sea salt

1½ cups [330 g] unsalted butter, at room temperature

2½ cups [500 g] granulated sugar

½ cup [100 g] firmly packed dark brown sugar

5 eggs, at room temperature

1¼ cups [300 ml] buttermilk

1 Tbsp vanilla extract

4 Tbsp [60 ml] Tennessee whiskey or bourbon

1½ cups [180 g] finely chopped toasted pecans (see page 16)

SALTED BUTTER–WHISKEY CARAMEL

1 cup [200 g] granulated sugar

2 Tbsp water

Pinch of cream of tartar

¾ cup [180 ml] heavy cream

4 Tbsp [60 g] salted butter

1 Tbsp Tennessee whiskey or bourbon

WHISKEY–BROWN SUGAR FROSTING

⅓ cup [45 g] all-purpose flour

1 cup [200 g] firmly packed dark brown sugar

1 cup [200g] granulated sugar

¼ tsp fine sea salt

1½ cups [360 ml] whole milk

1½ tsp vanilla extract

1½ cups [330 g] unsalted butter, at room temperature

1 to 2 Tbsp Tennessee whiskey or bourbon

BUTTERY PECANS

1 Tbsp salted butter

½ cup [60 g] pecan halves

Shot through with pecans and bathed in whiskey, caramel, and a hint of smoke, there is nothing shy about this spirited cake. It's frosted with an old-fashioned flour-thickened buttercream, called an ermine, or boiled-milk buttercream (see page 23). It starts with a thick pudding-like base that may remind you of kindergarten paste; if this type of frosting is new to you, there will probably come a point when you start doubting me, but have no fear! It goes from paste to perfection in just a few minutes. Don't refrigerate the buttercream, or it will never fully recapture its original creamy texture and might look curdled when you beat it again at room temperature. The whiskey syrup, caramel sauce, and pecans can all be made 2 or 3 days ahead of time. Store the nuts in a covered container at room temperature. Refrigerate the syrup and the caramel in covered containers and reheat gently to warm through right before using.

TENNESSEE WHISKEY PECAN CAKE

SERVES **8** TO **10**

Position a rack in the center of the oven. Preheat the oven to 350°F [180°C]. Coat three 9-in [23-cm] round cake pans with nonstick cooking spray and line the bottoms with parchment paper.

TO MAKE THE WHISKEY SYRUP: In a 3-qt [3-L] stainless-steel saucepan, combine the sugar, water, and butter over medium heat. Stir until the butter melts and the sugar dissolves. Increase the heat to high and bring to a boil. Cook for 1 to 2 minutes, until syrupy. Remove from heat and stir in the whiskey. Set aside.

TO MAKE THE CAKE: Sift together the flour, baking powder, baking soda, and salt into a large bowl. Set aside.

In the bowl of a stand mixer fitted with the paddle attachment, beat the butter and sugars together until light and creamy, 4 to 5 minutes. Scrape down the sides of the bowl. Beat in the eggs, one at a time, beating well after each addition.

Stir together the buttermilk, vanilla, and whiskey in a measuring cup with a pouring spout.

On low speed, beat one-third of the dry ingredients into the batter, just until the flour disappears, 10 to 15 seconds. Beat in half of the buttermilk mixture for a few seconds, just until combined. Add another one-third of the dry ingredients followed by the remaining buttermilk mixture. Finish by adding the final one-third of the dry ingredients, beating just until the batter is smooth. Fold the chopped pecans into the batter by hand using a rubber or silicone spatula.

Divide the batter evenly between the prepared pans, spreading the tops smooth with a spatula. Give each pan a little tap on the countertop to settle the batter. Bake for 25 to 30 minutes, until a wooden skewer inserted into the center of the cake comes out clean. Transfer the cakes to wire racks and let cool in the pans for 10 minutes. Invert the cake layers onto the racks, discarding the parchment paper.

While the cake layers are still warm, brush the tops and sides of each with warm whiskey syrup, making sure to use all the syrup. (If the syrup has cooled too much, warm it up a little over low heat, or for 10 to 20 seconds in the microwave, just until it is warm, before brushing on the cake.) Let cool completely.

TO MAKE THE CARAMEL: Combine the sugar, water, and cream of tartar in a 3-qt [3-L] stainless-steel saucepan over medium heat. Cook, gently swirling the pan occasionally but not stirring, until the sugar dissolves, about 2 to 3 minutes. Increase the heat to high and boil until the syrup turns a deep amber, the color of an old penny, 4 to 5 minutes. Watch carefully, as caramel can burn easily.

Remove the pan from the heat and pour in the cream, stirring with a long-handled wooden spoon, as the hot caramel has a tendency to hiss and splash when hit with the cold cream. Place the pan over low heat and cook for 3 to 4 minutes, stirring occasionally. Whisk in the salted butter, one tablespoon at a time, whisking each addition of butter into the caramel thoroughly before adding more. Remove from the heat and stir in the whiskey. Let cool to room temperature before using.

TO MAKE THE FROSTING: In a 3-qt [3-L] stainless-steel saucepan, whisk together the flour, sugars, and salt. Over medium-high heat, stir in the milk and cook, stirring constantly, until the sugars dissolve, 2 to 3 minutes. Increase the heat to high and bring the mixture to a vigorous boil, whisking continuously. Cook for 1½ to 2 minutes, until the liquid reduces to a very thick dense pudding. Don't skimp on the timing here—a minute is a lot longer than you think when you are whisking continuously—the pudding base needs enough cooking time to thicken properly. Set a timer if you are unsure.

Remove the pan from the heat and stir in the vanilla. Scrape into the bowl of a stand mixer fitted with the paddle attachment. Allow the mixture to cool completely until it is a very firm paste. (To speed up this process, you can refrigerate the mixture, uncovered, for up to 30 minutes. Don't be worried—it gets better looking.) With the mixer on low, start beating the cool pudding base to loosen it. Beat in the softened butter, 2 Tbsp at a time, adding more butter to the bowl after each addition is fully incorporated. When all the butter is incorporated, and the frosting is fluffy and light, beat in the

vanilla then the whiskey, 1 tsp at a time, making sure not to add so much that the frosting becomes too loose. It should be thick and very creamy. Use immediately, or cover and store at room temperature for up to 5 hours before using.

TO MAKE THE PECANS: Melt the butter in a small skillet or sauté pan until it is browned and bubbly. Add the pecans and stir the nuts to coat with the browned butter. Stir constantly over medium heat until the nuts are fragrant and crisp, about 1 minute. Pour onto a plate to cool. When cool, coarsely chop and reserve.

TO FINISH THE CAKE: Drizzle each cake layer with about ½ cup [160 g] of the lukewarm caramel, reserving ½ cup [160 g] to drizzle over the top of the frosted cake. When the caramel on the cake is completely cool and no longer tacky, start assembling the layers.

Place the first cake layer on a cake plate or cake stand and spread with 1 cup [200 g] frosting. Top with the second layer and spread with another 1 cup [200 g] frosting. Add the final cake layer and spread the top and sides of the cake with the remaining frosting. Refrigerate the cake until the frosting is cold and very firm, at least 30 minutes.

Warm the remaining ½ cup [160 g] caramel and drizzle it over the top of the cake. Arrange the chopped pecans in a loose pile in the center of the cake. Remove the cake from the refrigerator 1 to 2 hours before serving. Store the cake in a covered cake carrier or other container for up to 2 days.

GARDEN &
ORCHARD

I could devote an entire book to cakes inspired by a field trip to the farmers' market. Every season ushers in a fresh feast of colorful fruits and vegetables, and a smart baker knows when to step back and simplify, letting the flavors of each one take center stage with just an ever-so-gentle nudge—a little spice, a sprinkling of herbs, a splash of liqueur, or a dollop of cream—to help them shine their brightest.

In the fall, there are juicy pears, mild and sweet, that I will grate and fold into thick pound cake batter flavored with a sprinkling of woodsy rosemary and fresh lemon zest instead of the usual cinnamon and nutmeg. I will save those homey aromatics for an easy apple-walnut bundt cake made with fresh Pink Lady applesauce and drizzled with a crisp apple cider–caramel glaze. Balmy spring weather ushers in crimson stalks of rhubarb that I'll roast in the oven with fresh ginger-and-orange-infused sugar. Once the compote cools, I'll use it to sandwich together sturdy layers of Victoria Sponge (page 163) from a recipe I learned to make so many years ago in cooking school. In the summer, there are juicy nectarines to slice and bake into an old-fashioned crumble-topped buckle, plums for a buttery carda-mom-spiced almond cake, and ripe raspberries to dot atop a brown butter-infused French Financier cake (page 160). A single layer of luscious, golden buttermilk cake is the perfect foundation for an abundance of fresh ber-ries from dusky blues to juicy blackberries, spilling over a jaunty turban of whipped cream streaked with rosy ribbons of strawberries simmered into a thick, jammy compote (page 158).

Delicately flavored, this simple loaf gets a mild, savory edge from the addition of rosemary and a little olive oil. Two teaspoons of finely minced rosemary gives the cake a subtle, herbal quality, but if you want a more pungent flavor and aroma, increase the rosemary to 3 teaspoons. For added texture, consider leaving the pear unpeeled before grating it. This cake ages well, becoming more flavorful the day after it's baked.

PEAR, LEMON & ROSEMARY CAKE

SERVES 6 TO 8

1½ cups [210 g] all-purpose flour

1½ tsp baking powder

½ tsp fine sea salt

½ cup [110 g] unsalted butter, at room temperature

¼ cup [60 ml] light olive oil (not extra-virgin, it is too strongly flavored)

1 cup [200 g] granulated sugar

1 tsp grated lemon zest

3 eggs, at room temperature

⅓ cup [80 g] plain Greek yogurt

1 tsp vanilla extract

2 to 3 tsp very finely minced fresh rosemary (see recipe introduction)

1 large, ripe-but-firm pear, peeled, cored, and grated (about 1 cup [200 to 230 g])

2 Tbsp pear eau-de-vie or pear brandy

Demerara or raw sugar for sprinkling

Position a rack in the center of the oven. Preheat the oven to 350°F [180°C]. Coat a 9-in-by-5-in [23-cm-by-13-cm] metal loaf pan with nonstick cooking spray. Line the pan with an 8½-by-15-in [21.5-by-38-cm] strip of parchment paper so it covers the bottom of the pan and hangs over the long sides.

Sift together the flour, baking powder, and salt into a small bowl. Set aside.

In a large bowl, beat together the butter, olive oil, sugar, and lemon zest with an electric mixer set at medium speed until light and fluffy, 3 to 4 minutes. Add the eggs, one at a time, beating well after each addition. Beat in the yogurt, vanilla, and rosemary.

Fold in the dry ingredients by hand with a rubber or silicone spatula until smooth. Gently fold the grated pear and pear eau de vie into the batter, just until combined.

Scrape the batter into the prepared pan and smooth the top. Sprinkle with the demerara sugar. Bake for 45 to 50 minutes, until a wooden skewer inserted into the center of the cake comes out clean.

Set the loaf, still in the pan, on a wire rack and let cool for 10 minutes. Grasping the overhanging parchment, lift the loaf out of the pan and set it on the rack. Let cool completely, discarding the parchment paper. When cool, cut into thick slices.

The cake will keep, well wrapped in plastic wrap, at room temperature for up to 3 days.

This rich almond butter cake can also be made with fresh berries or stone fruit like peaches or nectarines, but I think it is especially lovely made with plums and spiced with cardamom. The recipe comes from my friend Vivian Hernandez-Jackson, who owns the charming Cuban-style patisserie, Azucar, in San Diego.

PLUM-CARDAMOM CAKE

SERVES 8

1 cup [220 g] unsalted butter
1 cup [200 g] sugar, plus 1 Tbsp
3 oz [85 g] almond paste
2 eggs
1 tsp vanilla extract
½ tsp almond extract
1 cup [120 g] cake flour
½ cup [70 g] all-purpose flour
1¼ tsp baking powder
¼ tsp ground cardamom
⅛ tsp ground nutmeg
½ tsp fine sea salt
4 or 5 firm plums, halved and pitted
¼ to ⅓ cup [25 g to 35 g] sliced almonds
Confectioners' sugar for sprinkling

Position a rack in the center of the oven. Preheat the oven to 350°F [180°C]. Coat a 9-in [23-cm] round cake pan with nonstick cooking spray and line the bottom with parchment paper.

In a stand mixer fitted with the paddle attachment, beat together the butter, the 1 cup sugar, and the almond paste on medium speed for 3 to 5 minutes, until well combined and fluffy.

Add the eggs, one at a time, beating well after each addition. Beat in the vanilla and almond extracts. Scrape down the sides of the bowl.

Sift the flours, baking powder, cardamom, nutmeg, and salt into the bowl. Using a rubber or silicone spatula, fold in the dry ingredients just until smooth. Scrape the batter into the prepared pan, spreading the top evenly with a spatula.

Slice each plum half into 3 wedges and arrange them decoratively on top of the batter, pressing them in gently. Sprinkle with the sliced almonds and the 1 Tbsp granulated sugar.

Bake for 25 to 27 minutes, until a wooden skewer inserted into the center of the cake comes out clean. Let cool completely in the pan on a wire rack. When the cake is cool, run a knife around the edges of the pan to loosen the cake, if necessary, and invert it onto the rack. Remove the pan and discard the parchment paper. Place a cake plate over the cake and invert again so the cake is on the plate plum-side up. Sprinkle lightly with confectioners' sugar. Cut into wedges and serve. This cake is best served the day it is made.

4 large Pink Lady apples, peeled, cored, and diced

1 cup [240 ml] unfiltered apple cider

1 Tbsp apple cider vinegar

2 tsp ground cinnamon

3 cups [420 g] all-purpose flour

1½ tsp baking powder

1 tsp baking soda

1¼ tsp fine sea salt

½ tsp freshly grated nutmeg

½ tsp ground allspice

¼ tsp ground cloves

¼ tsp ground cardamom

¾ cup [165 g] unsalted butter, at room temperature

½ cup [120 ml] canola oil

1¼ cups [250 g] granulated sugar

1¼ cups [250 g] firmly packed dark brown sugar

1 tsp vanilla extract

4 eggs, at room temperature

2 cups [240 g] pecan halves, coarsely chopped and toasted (see page 16)

APPLE CIDER–CARAMEL GLAZE

2 Tbsp unfiltered apple cider

½ cup [100 g] granulated sugar

½ tsp ground cinnamon

½ cup [120 ml] heavy cream

2 Tbsp unsalted butter

Pinch of fine sea salt

1 to 2 Tbsp applejack, Calvados, or other apple brandy (optional)

1 cup [120 g] confectioners' sugar, measured and then sifted

Save baking this cake for the perfect fall day, when the air is crisp, when local apples and fresh-pressed cider grab the spotlight at farmers' markets, and roadside stands are bursting with autumn's bounty. Make sure to cook the apple purée down until it is very thick, almost dry, for the most intense, concentrated apple flavor.

PINK LADY APPLESAUCE CAKE
WITH APPLE CIDER– CARAMEL GLAZE

SERVES 10 TO 12

In a 3-qt [2.8-L] saucepan, stir together the diced apples, apple cider, apple cider vinegar, and 1 tsp of the cinnamon and cook, covered, over medium heat until the apples are soft and almost translucent, 15 to 20 minutes. Uncover and cook, stirring occasionally to keep from sticking, until the apples are completely broken down and the sauce has cooked down to about 1 cup [225 g] of very thick, dense purée. Remove from the heat and let cool completely.

Position a rack in the center of the oven. Preheat the oven to 350°F [180°C]. Coat a 10-cup [2.4-L] Bundt pan with nonstick cooking spray.

In a medium bowl, sift together the flour, baking powder, baking soda, salt, the remaining 1 tsp cinnamon, the nutmeg, allspice, cloves, and cardamom. Set aside.

In the bowl of a stand mixer fitted with the paddle attachment, beat together the butter, oil, granulated sugar, and dark brown sugar until creamy, 3 to 4 minutes. Beat in the vanilla and the eggs, one at a time, beating well after each addition. Beat in the cooled applesauce. Add the dry ingredients and beat for a few seconds, just until the batter is smooth. Use a rubber or silicone spatula to fold the nuts into the batter by hand.

Scrape the batter into the prepared pan and bake for 55 to 65 minutes, until a wooden skewer inserted into the center of the cake comes out clean. Transfer the cake to a wire rack and let cool for 10 to 15 minutes. Turn the cake out onto the rack and let cool completely.

TO MAKE THE GLAZE: While the cake is baking, combine the apple cider, granulated sugar, and cinnamon in a 3-qt [2.8-L] heavy-bottomed saucepan over medium heat. Cook, gently swirling the pan occasionally without stirring, until the sugar dissolves and starts to change color. Increase the heat to high and boil until the syrup turns a deep amber (the color of an old penny), 4 to 5 minutes. (Watch carefully, as the syrup can burn easily.)

Immediately remove the pan from the heat and stir in the cream with a long-handled wooden spoon. Be careful to avoid splattering, as the caramel will bubble furiously at first when combined with the cream. Decrease the heat to medium-low and cook, stirring constantly, until the caramel thickens, 3 to 5 minutes. Remove the sauce from the heat and whisk in the butter, salt, and apple brandy until smooth. Whisk in the confectioners' sugar. Let the glaze sit, stirring occasionally, until it is lukewarm but still pourable.

Transfer the cake to a serving plate or cake stand. Pour the warm glaze over the top of the cake, allowing it to drip down the sides. Store the cake in a covered cake carrier or other container at room temperature for up to 3 days.

If you look up "buckle" in the dictionary, it means "to bend, warp, bulge, or collapse." That's exactly what happens as this nectarine buckle bakes and the cake valiantly rises under the heavy burden of fruit and streusel it carries. Buckled and cobbled, juicy and crunchy, all in one sweet mouthful, it's perfect warm, or at room temperature, at any time of day.

SUMMER NECTARINE BUCKLE

SERVES 8

3 large ripe-but-firm nectarines, halved, pitted, and cut into ½-in [12-mm] wedges

1 Tbsp apricot schnapps or brandy

1½ cups [210 g] all-purpose flour

¼ cup [30 g] almond flour or almond meal

2 tsp baking powder

¾ tsp fine sea salt

½ tsp freshly grated nutmeg

¾ cup [220 g] unsalted butter, at room temperature

1¼ cups [250 g] sugar

3 eggs, at room temperature

2 tsp vanilla extract

¼ tsp almond extract

¼ cup [60 g] sour cream or plain whole-milk yogurt

CRUMBLE

¾ cup [150 g] firmly packed dark brown sugar

¾ cup [105 g] all-purpose flour

⅓ cup [35 g] sliced almonds

¼ tsp fine sea salt

6 tablespoons [110 g] unsalted butter, melted

Position a rack in the center of the oven. Preheat the oven to 350°F [180°C]. Grease a 10-in [25-cm] round cast-iron skillet or 9-in [23-cm] springform pan.

In a medium bowl, toss the nectarine wedges with the apricot schnapps. Set aside.

In a medium bowl, whisk together the all-purpose flour, almond flour, baking powder, salt, and nutmeg. Set aside.

In a medium bowl, with a hand mixer, beat the butter and sugar together at medium speed until light and creamy, 3 to 4 minutes. Beat in the eggs, one at a time, beating well after each addition. Beat in the vanilla, almond extract, and sour cream. Beat the dry ingredients into the batter in three additions, beating just until smooth, 10 to 15 seconds, after each addition.

Scrape the batter into the prepared pan and spread the top evenly with a spatula. Arrange the dressed nectarines decoratively in an even layer over the batter.

TO MAKE THE CRUMBLE: In a large bowl, with a fork, stir together the brown sugar, flour, sliced almonds, and salt. Stir in the melted butter until the mixture forms soft, moist, pebbly crumbs. Sprinkle the crumble evenly over the nectarines.

Bake for 45 to 50 minutes, until a wooden skewer inserted into the center of the cake comes out clean. Let cool slightly before slicing and serving straight from the skillet.

This cake is best served the day it is made.

158

Cooking strawberries into a syrupy, almost jam-like purée intensifies their flavor and color, and is beautiful swirled into the whipped cream piled atop this cake. Adding a splash of St. Germain—a delicate liqueur distilled from hand-picked elderflowers—delivers subtle hints of lychee, pear, and stone fruit and enhances the ripe mixed berry topping's naturally sweet perfume.

SUMMER BERRY ST. GERMAIN CAKE

SERVES 8

STRAWBERRY PURÉE

2 cups [280 g] sliced fresh strawberries or frozen strawberries, thawed

2 Tbsp freshly squeezed orange juice

2 Tbsp sugar

LEMON-BUTTERMILK CAKE

1¾ cups [245 g] all-purpose flour

2 tsp baking powder

½ tsp fine sea salt

1¼ cups [250 g] sugar

1 tsp grated lemon zest

¾ cup [165 g] unsalted butter, at room temperature, cut into pieces

2 eggs, at room temperature

1 tsp vanilla extract

2 Tbsp freshly squeezed lemon juice

⅔ cup [160 ml] buttermilk or whole-milk yogurt

BERRY TOPPING

¼ cup [50 g] sugar

1 Tbsp lemon juice

2 Tbsp St. Germain liqueur

1½ pints [360 g] mixed berries (such as raspberries, blackberries, blueberries, and/or sliced strawberries)

1 cup [240 ml] chilled heavy cream

½ cup [120 g] chilled crème fraîche

¼ cup sugar, plus more if needed

2 or 3 pink organically grown rosebuds for garnish

1 or 2 sprigs fresh mint for garnish

TO MAKE THE PURÉE: In a medium saucepan, stir together the sliced strawberries, orange juice, and sugar over medium-high heat. Cover and bring to a gentle boil, stirring occasionally, until the sugar dissolves and the strawberries release their juices and start to soften. Decrease the heat to medium-low and cook for 3 to 4 more minutes, until the mixture thickens and the juices become syrupy. Remove from the heat. Purée in a blender or food processor. Scrape the purée into a container, cover, and refrigerate until cold, at least 1 hour or up to 1 day ahead of serving.

Position a rack in the center of the oven. Preheat the oven to 350°F [180°C]. Coat a 9-in [23-cm] round cake pan or springform pan with nonstick cooking spray and line the bottom with parchment paper.

TO MAKE THE CAKE: In a small bowl, sift together the flour, baking powder, and salt. Set aside.

In a stand mixer fitted with the paddle attachment, combine the sugar and lemon zest and rub together with your fingertips until the sugar is moist and sandy and fragrant with lemon. Beat the lemon sugar and butter together on medium speed until light and creamy, 3 to 4 minutes. Add the eggs, one at a time, beating well after each addition. Beat in the vanilla and lemon juice. Scrape down the sides of the bowl.

With the mixer on low speed, add the dry ingredients in two additions, alternating with the buttermilk in two additions, beginning and ending with dry ingredients and beating just until the batter is smooth, 10 to 15 seconds after each.

Scrape the batter into the prepared pan, smoothing the top with a spatula. Bake for 30 to 35 minutes, until a wooden skewer inserted into the center of the cake comes out clean.

Transfer to a wire rack and let cool in the pan for 10 minutes. Invert the cake onto the rack, discard the parchment paper, and let cool completely. (At this point the cake can be wrapped well in plastic wrap and stored at room temperature for up to 2 days.)

TO MAKE THE TOPPING: In a medium bowl, stir together the sugar, the lemon juice, and the St. Germain liqueur. Add the mixed berries and toss to coat with the syrup. Cover and refrigerate the compote until ready to spoon over the cake.

Chill a metal mixing bowl and the beaters of a hand mixer for 15 minutes. Combine the cream, crème fraîche, and sugar in the bowl and beat on medium-high speed until soft, thick, spoonable peaks form. Taste for sweetness and add 1 or 2 tablespoons more sugar if you prefer a sweeter cream. With a rubber or silicone spatula, gently fold the cold strawberry purée into with the whipped cream once or twice, just enough to give it a swirled effect.

TO FINISH THE CAKE: Right before serving, place the cake, top-side up, on a cake plate or cake stand. Pile the cream on top of the cake. Spoon the berry compote on top of the cream.

Garnish with one or two pink rose buds and a sprig or two of fresh mint. Serve immediately, or refrigerate for up to 1 hour to keep the whipped cream fresh.

Every respectable pastry shop in France carries *financiers*—dense, buttery little cakes made with ground almonds and baked in small rectangular molds shaped like gold ingots. Although bite-size confections are traditional, the batter translates well to a larger cake, and is especially pretty when baked in a fluted tart pan, as in this version. Make sure to refrigerate the batter for a few hours before baking, and preferably overnight, as this improves the texture of the cake.

RASPBERRY-HAZELNUT FINANCIER

SERVES 8 TO 10

1 cup [220 g] unsalted butter

1 cup [120 g] ground hazelnut flour or meal

1 cup [120 g] ground almond flour or meal

1½ cups [180 g] confectioners' sugar, measured then sifted

¾ cup [150 g] granulated sugar

8 egg whites, at room temperature

2 Tbsp Frangelico or other hazelnut liqueur

1 tsp vanilla extract

¼ tsp almond extract

¾ cup [105 g] all-purpose flour

½ tsp fine sea salt

1 pint [240 g] fresh raspberries

¼ cup [75 g] apricot jam, melted and strained

Melt the butter in a medium saucepan over low heat. When the butter is completely melted, increase the heat to high and bring the butter to a boil. Continue cooking, stirring constantly with a wooden spoon, until the boiling subsides and the milk solids in the butter start to turn brown. As the milk solids brown and caramelize, the butter will develop a sweet, slightly nutty aroma. This should take 5 to 7 minutes. Immediately pour the brown butter into a heatproof bowl to stop cooking and allow it to cool slightly.

In a separate bowl, using a wooden spoon, stir together the hazelnut meal, almond meal, confectioners' sugar, and granulated sugar. Stir in the egg whites, Frangelico, vanilla, and almond extract just until smooth and combined. Sift the flour and salt into the batter and fold in gently

with a rubber or silicone spatula. Gently fold the cooled brown butter into the batter. Cover the bowl with plastic wrap and refrigerate until the batter is cold and firm, at least 2 hours and preferably overnight.

Position a rack in the center of the oven. Preheat the oven to 425°F [220°C]. Coat a 9½-in [24-cm] or 10½-in [26.5-cm] fluted tart pan with a removable bottom with nonstick cooking spray.

Scrape the batter into the prepared pan, spreading it smooth with a spatula. Dot the top of the batter with the raspberries. Bake for 10 minutes, then decrease the heat to 375°F [190°C] and continue baking for another 25 to 30 minutes (this will depend on the size of the tart pan you use), until a wooden skewer inserted into

Continued

the center of the cake comes out clean or with only a few moist crumbs clinging to it. Transfer to a wire rack and let cool for at least 10 minutes before removing the cake from the tart pan. Unmold the cake and place on a cake platter. Brush the top with the warm apricot jam.

Although best eaten the day it is baked, the cake can be stored at room temperature in a covered cake carrier or other container for up to 2 days.

One of my favorite guilty pleasures is spending a lazy afternoon watching British murder mysteries on TV. It's bizarrely comforting to watch English country folk in the (happily) fictional rural villages of Badger's Drift, Elverton-cum-Latterly, or St. Mary Mead discern ever more elaborate methods of rubbing each other out. If you're interested in indulging your inner Miss Marple, this classic Victoria sponge, sandwiched thickly with cream and crimson chunks of roasted rhubarb, is just the ticket. Mystery writer Agatha Christie adored the thick, buttery cream of her native Devon in southern England, and often kept a large mug of it near her typewriter, taking quick nips to sustain her as she wrote. Look for hothouse, or "forced," rhubarb when you can. It has a deeper, more crimson color than field-grown rhubarb, and will retain its vibrant, rosy color even when roasted.

PROPER VICTORIA SPONGE
WITH GINGER-ROASTED RHUBARB AND DEVONSHIRE-STYLE CREAM

SERVES 8

1 cup [220 g] unsalted butter, at room temperature

1¼ cups [250 g] granulated sugar

Grated zest of 1 lemon

4 eggs, at room temperature

1½ tsp vanilla extract

1⅔ cups [230 g] all-purpose flour

2 tsp baking powder

1 tsp fine sea salt

2 to 3 Tbsp whole milk

GINGER-ROASTED RHUBARB

1 lb [455 g] very pink, fresh rhubarb cut into 2-in [5-cm] pieces

⅔ cup [130 g] granulated sugar

1 tsp grated orange zest

One 1½-in [4-cm] chunk fresh ginger, peeled and grated

DEVONSHIRE-STYLE CREAM

1 cup [240 ml] very cold heavy cream

⅓ to ½ cup [40 to 60 g] confectioners' sugar, plus more for sprinkling over the cake

8 oz [240 g] mascarpone cheese, at room temperature

1 tsp vanilla extract

⅓ cup [100 g] jam of your choice: strawberry-rhubarb, strawberry, or seedless raspberry

Confectioners' sugar for sprinkling

Position a rack in the center of the oven. Preheat the oven to 350°F [180°C]. Coat two 9-in [23-cm] round cake pans with nonstick cooking spray. Line the bottoms with parchment paper.

In a stand mixer fitted with the paddle attachment, beat the butter until creamy, about 1 minute. Combine the sugar and lemon zest in a small bowl and rub the sugar and zest together with your fingertips until the sugar is moist and sandy and fragrant with lemon. Add the lemon sugar to the bowl and beat on medium-high until combined. Add the eggs, one at a time, beating well after each addition. Beat in the vanilla.

Sift the flour, baking powder, and salt into the batter and fold in by hand with a rubber or silicone spatula. Fold in the milk.

Divide the batter equally between the prepared pans, spreading it evenly with a spatula.

Continued

Bake for 17 to 20 minutes, until a wooden skewer inserted into the center of the cake comes out clean.

Let the cakes cool in their pans on wire racks for 10 minutes. Invert the cake layers onto the racks, discard the parchment paper, and let cool completely.

TO MAKE THE RHUBARB: Preheat the oven to 400°F [190°C].

Spread the rhubarb pieces in a single layer on a 9-by-13-in [23-by 33-cm] rimmed baking pan. Combine the sugar, orange zest, and ginger in a small bowl and rub the sugar together with the orange zest and ginger until the sugar is moist and sandy and fragrant. Sprinkle the infused sugar over the rhubarb. Roast the rhubarb until tender and starting to release its juices, 15 to 20 minutes.

Remove the rhubarb from the oven and let cool completely. Carefully transfer the rhubarb with a slotted spatula to a clean dish. Pour any cooking juices from the pan into a small saucepan and simmer over medium heat until syrupy, 3 to 5 minutes. Remove the syrup from the heat and let cool completely. Pour the syrup over the roasted rhubarb and refrigerate until ready to assemble the cake.

TO MAKE THE DEVONSHIRE-STYLE CREAM: Using a food processor fitted with the metal blade, whip the cold cream with ⅓ cup [40 g] of the confectioners' sugar, using short pulses, until it thickens very slightly, about 1 minute. (Cream whipped in the food processor is denser and less fluffy than cream whipped with an electric mixer.) Add the mascarpone and vanilla and give the cream 1 or 2 short pulses, just to combine. The cream should be thick and dense but still spreadable. Take care not to overmix the cream and mascarpone, or the mixture will be grainy. Taste for sweetness, and if a sweeter cream is desired, add the remaining confectioners' sugar to taste, 1 tsp at a time.

TO FINISH THE CAKE: Place one cake layer on a cake platter or cake stand. Spread a thin layer of jam over the top of the cake and then spread thickly with the Devonshire cream. Top the cream with the roasted rhubarb and drizzle with the reduced rhubarb syrup. Top with the second layer of cake and sprinkle with confectioners' sugar or top with another layer of jam, Devonshire cream, and roasted rhubarb, if you have extra. Serve immediately, or refrigerate for up to 1 hour to keep the whipped cream fresh.

2 cups [260 g] all-purpose flour

½ cup [70 g] whole-wheat pastry flour

2 tsp baking powder

½ tsp baking soda

1 tsp fine sea salt

1 Tbsp ground cinnamon

1 tsp freshly grated nutmeg

½ tsp ground allspice

4 eggs

1½ cups [300 g] firmly packed light brown sugar

1½ cups [300 g] granulated sugar

1 cup [240 ml] canola or vegetable oil

½ cup [110 g] unsalted butter, melted

2 tsp vanilla extract

1 lb [450 g] carrots, peeled and grated

1 large sweet apple, such as Fuji, Gala, or
   Honeycrisp, peeled, cored, and grated

1 cup [120 g] chopped walnuts or pecans,
   toasted (see page 16)

1½ cups [90 g] sweetened flaked coconut

CREAM CHEESE FROSTING

1 lb [455 g] cream cheese, at room temperature

¾ cup [165 g] unsalted butter, at room
   temperature

2 tsp vanilla extract

6 to 8 cups [720 to 960 g] confectioners' sugar

¼ cup [55 g] plain Greek yogurt

Perhaps I should have called this cake the Chunky Bunny. Carrot cake is an old-time favorite, and I think the richer and *chunkier* the batter, the better. Here it's stuffed with lots of nuts, coconut, and freshly grated carrots, with grated sweet apple thrown in for good measure. I always add a touch of whole-wheat flour to my carrot cake for a little added heft and nuttiness, but you can substitute an equal amount of all-purpose flour if you prefer. Carrot cake can sometimes be dense and oily, so to lighten things up a touch, instead of stirring all the ingredients together by hand, I beat the eggs and sugar together until they are fluffy, and then drizzle in the oil and melted butter. This forms an emulsion similar in texture to mayonnaise, delivering a slightly more refined texture without sacrificing any of the cake's original "chunky" appeal.

CHUBBY BUNNY

SERVES **8** TO **10**

Position a rack in the center of the oven. Preheat the oven to 350°F [180°C]. Coat three 8-in [20-cm] or 9-in [23-cm] round cake pans with nonstick cooking spray and line the bottoms with parchment paper.

Sift the flours, baking powder, baking soda, salt, cinnamon, nutmeg, and allspice into a large bowl. Set aside.

In the bowl of a stand mixer fitted with the paddle attachment, combine the eggs and sugars and beat on medium-high speed until light and fluffy, about 4 minutes. With the mixer running, drizzle in the oil and melted butter, beating just until combined. Beat in the vanilla. With the mixer on low, beat in the dry ingredients, just until combined. With a large rubber spatula, fold in the grated carrots, grated apple, walnuts, and coconut.

Divide the batter evenly between the prepared pans, spreading the tops smooth with a spatula. Bake for 30 to 40 minutes, until a wooden skewer inserted into the center of the cake comes out clean and the edges start to pull away from the sides of the cake pans.

Transfer the cakes to wire racks and let cool in the pans for 10 minutes. Unmold onto the racks and discard the parchment paper. Let cool completely.

TO MAKE THE FROSTING: In a stand mixer fitted with the paddle attachment, beat the cream cheese and butter together until creamy, 2 to 3 minutes. Beat in the vanilla. Sift 6 cups [720 g] of the confectioners' sugar into the butter mixture and beat until smooth. Beat in the yogurt. If the frosting is too thin, beat in 1 to 2 cups

Continued

[120 to 240 g] more sifted confectioners' sugar until thick and spreadable.

TO FINISH THE CAKE: Place one cake layer on a cake stand or cake plate and spread with 1 heaping cup [260 g] of the frosting. Top with the second layer and spread with another 1 cup [260 g] of frosting, Top with the final cake layer and frost the top and sides of the cake generously with the remaining frosting.

Refrigerate the cake in a covered cake carrier or other container for up to 2 days. When ready to serve, let the cake sit at room temperature for about 1 hour before slicing.

A rose by any other name would be a . . . strawberry. Strawberries are a distant member of the rose family, which might explain their intoxicating fragrance when perfectly ripe. If romance is on your mind, forgo the flowers and make this cake instead. Freeze-dried strawberries, crushed to a fine powder, add an intense pop of concentrated berry flavor and bright color when combined with the fresh fruit in the Strawberry-Cheesecake Frosting.

CHOCOLATE-DIPPED STRAWBERRY CAKE

SERVES 8 TO 10

2 cups [280 g] all-purpose flour

¾ cup [60 g] natural cocoa powder (see page 13)

1 tsp baking powder

1 tsp baking soda

¼ tsp fine sea salt

2 cups [400 g] granulated sugar

2 eggs

1 tsp instant espresso powder or instant coffee granules

2 tsp vanilla extract

1 cup [240 g] mayonnaise

1⅓ cups [320 ml] boiling water

STRAWBERRY-CHEESECAKE FROSTING

½ cup [110 g] unsalted butter, at room temperature

1 lb [455 g] cream cheese, at room temperature

1 tsp vanilla extract

6 to 8 cups [720 g to 960 g] confectioners' sugar, measured then sifted

½ to ¾ cup [100 to 150 g] fresh strawberries, stemmed and very finely chopped

One 1.2-oz bag [34 g] freeze-dried strawberries, crushed to a fine powder

CHOCOLATE-DIPPED STRAWBERRIES

10 perfect strawberries, at room temperature (cold berries might release condensation, and the moisture will cause the chocolate to seize and prevent it from sticking to the berries.)

½ cup [90 g] semisweet chocolate chips

Fresh whole and halved strawberries, coarsely crumbled freeze-dried strawberries, chopped pistachios (optional)

Position a rack in the center of the oven. Preheat the oven to 350°F [180°C]. Coat two 9-in [23-cm] round cake pans with nonstick cooking spray and line the bottoms with parchment paper.

In a medium bowl, sift together the flour, cocoa powder, baking powder, baking soda, and salt.

In the bowl of a stand mixer fitted with the paddle attachment, beat together the sugar, eggs, and espresso powder at medium-high speed until light and fluffy, 3 to 4 minutes. Beat in the vanilla. Add the mayonnaise to the egg mixture and beat on medium speed until smooth.

Decrease the mixer speed to its lowest setting and beat in half of the dry ingredients just until combined. Stop the mixer and scrape down the sides of the bowl.

Add half of the boiling water to the batter and beat on low speed just until the batter is smooth, 5 to 10 seconds. Add the remaining dry ingredients and beat just

until combined. Add the remaining boiling water and beat just until smooth. The batter will be somewhat thin.

Divide the batter evenly between the prepared pans and smooth the tops with a spatula. Bake for 20 to 25 minutes, until a wooden skewer inserted into the middle of each cake comes out clean. Transfer the cake layers to wire racks and let cool in their pans for 10 minutes. Invert the cakes onto the racks and discard the parchment paper. Let cool completely. While the cake is cooling, prepare the frosting.

TO MAKE THE FROSTING: In the bowl of a stand mixer fitted with the paddle attachment, beat the butter and cream cheese together until fluffy, 1 to 2 minutes. Scrape down the sides of the bowl and beat in the vanilla. Beat in 6 cups [720 g] of the confectioners' sugar until smooth. Beat in the fresh and powdered freeze-dried strawberries. Beat until smooth (there will be tiny flecks of strawberry

Continued

throughout the frosting). If a firmer consistency is desired, beat in additional confectioners' sugar, adding it ½ cup [60 g] at a time. Set aside.

TO MAKE THE CHOCOLATE-DIPPED STRAWBERRIES: Line a plate or baking sheet with parchment paper. Pat the berries with a dry paper towel to absorb any excess moisture. Place the chocolate chips in a microwave-safe bowl and microwave on high for 1 minute. Stir the chocolate chips. Return to the microwave and microwave in 15-second increments, stirring with a wooden spoon between each, until the chocolate is melted and smooth. Transfer the chocolate to a small, deep, custard cup. Working with one strawberry at a time, dip a strawberry halfway into the chocolate. Hold the dipped berry over the custard cup, shaking off any excess chocolate. Place the berry on the prepared plate or baking sheet to harden. Dip the remaining 9 berries in chocolate. Let harden at room temperature (or to hurry the process, refrigerate until you need the berries to decorate the cake. The berries can be refrigerated, uncovered, in a single layer without touching for up to 8 hours).

TO FINISH THE CAKE: Place one cake layer on a cake plate or cake stand, and frost with 1 heaping cup [260 g] of the frosting. Top with the second cake layer and frost the top and sides generously with the remaining frosting and smooth with an offset spatula.

Fit a 16-in [40.5-cm] disposable piping bag with a large star tip and fill halfway with strawberry frosting. Pipe rosettes of frosting all over the top of the cake. Decorate with chocolate-dipped strawberries and fresh whole and halved strawberries on some of the rosettes of buttercream.

Refrigerate in a covered cake carrier for up to 2 days.

ACKNOWLEDGMENTS

I love my team at Chronicle Books. Thank you all for your talent and creativity, it always delights me. Heartfelt thanks go to my amazing editor, Amy Treadwell, who took this book under her wing and gave it a home (and always answered my calls). Big hugs to my design team, including senior designer Alice Chau, photographer Leigh Beisch, food stylist Robyn Valarik, prop stylist Sara Slavin, and to illustrator Jordan Sondler. you have infused this book with so much personality and charm. Many thanks to editor Sarah Billingsley, who after all of our brainstorming and many discarded ideas, came up with the absolutely perfect title for this book.

Thank you to my agent Jenni Ferrari-Adler for her advice and encouragement.

If I were to land on a deserted island with only one dessert to console me, it would have to be cake. I am so lucky to know so many equally enthusiastic cake lovers who agreed to taste and recipe test for me. My thanks go to:

Seth and Veronica Reek, Adam and Sandy Reek, Ethan, Jillian, Dario, and Ava, the big, beautiful O'Connor clan, Mardi Barron, Judi Farwell, Scott Frazer, Sally Pasley Vargas, Denise Marchessault, Sheri Castle, Linda Nygard, Heather Walker, Sue Ratzer, Laura Mancuso, Paul Horne, Tricia McCormick, Deb O'Connor, Liz Goedde Jamero, Betsey McKnight Signol, Domenica Marchetti, Debbie Koenig, Selena Darrow, Terry Paetzold, Joanne Fabish, Liz Tarpy, Mary Ann Kelly, and my friends at the *San Diego Union Tribune*: Chris Ross, Ani Arambula, and Eduardo Contreras. Special thanks go to Toni Burnett-Rands who befriended me through social media and agreed to test many recipes all the way from Hobart, Tasmania. It's been a treat and a privilege.

Thank you to the wonderful bakers in my life who shared their recipes with me: my late great-grandmother, Alline Robideaux, who handed her recipes down to my mother who shared them with me; to Heather Nunnelly, who diligently tested recipes and shared her grandma's special Banana Bourbon Stack Cake, and to Vivian Hernandez-Jackson, owner of Azucar bakery in San Diego, for sharing the recipe for her delicate and luscious fruit-topped almond cake.

As always, thanks to dear friends and fellow cook book authors, Nancie McDermott, Robin Asbell, Susan Russo, Jamie Schler, Sandra Gutierrez, Cheryl Sternman Rule, Tara Mataraza Desmond, Ivy Manning, and Denise Vivaldo, for listening and advising and all-around hand-holding when I needed it, and for testing a recipe "just one more time" no matter how messy it made your kitchen. And to Sandi Burke, Cambi Martin, and Lynell Sanchez for keeping me sane and eating my failures.

As always, my heart belongs to my beautiful, cake-loving family who cheer me on every day: My wonderful mom, who let me loose in the kitchen so long ago and today entrusts me with her special family recipes; my husband Jim and our daughters Olivia and Sophia—and of course, Charlotte—who thinks I am wonderful no matter what I do.

INDEX